WHEN POETRY RULED THE STREETS

WHEN POETRY RULED THE STREETS

The French May Events of 1968

Andrew Feenberg and Jim Freedman
with a foreword by Douglas Kellner

State University of New York Press

Published by
State University of New York Press, Albany

For information, address State University of New York Press
90 State Street, Suite 700, Albany, New York, 12207

Production by Dana Foote
Marketing by Fran Keneston

Library of Congress Cataloging-in-Publication Data

Feenberg, Andrew.
When poetry ruled the streets : the French May events of 1968 /
Andrew Feenberg and Jim Freedman ; with a foreword by Douglas Kellner.
p. cm.
Includes bibliographical references and index.
ISBN 0–7914–4965–3 (alk. paper)—ISBN 0–7914–4966–1 (pbk. : alk. paper)
1. Riots—France—Paris—History—20th century. 2. College students—
France—Political activity—History—20th century. 3. Working class—France—
Paris—Political activity—History—20th century. 4. General Strike, France,
1968. 5. Paris (France)—History—1944– 6. France—Politics and government—
1958– 7. Radicalism—France—History—20th century.
I. Freedman, Jim, 1944– II. Title.

DC420 .F44 2001
944'.36—dc21
2001018877

10 9 8 7 6 5 4 3 2 1

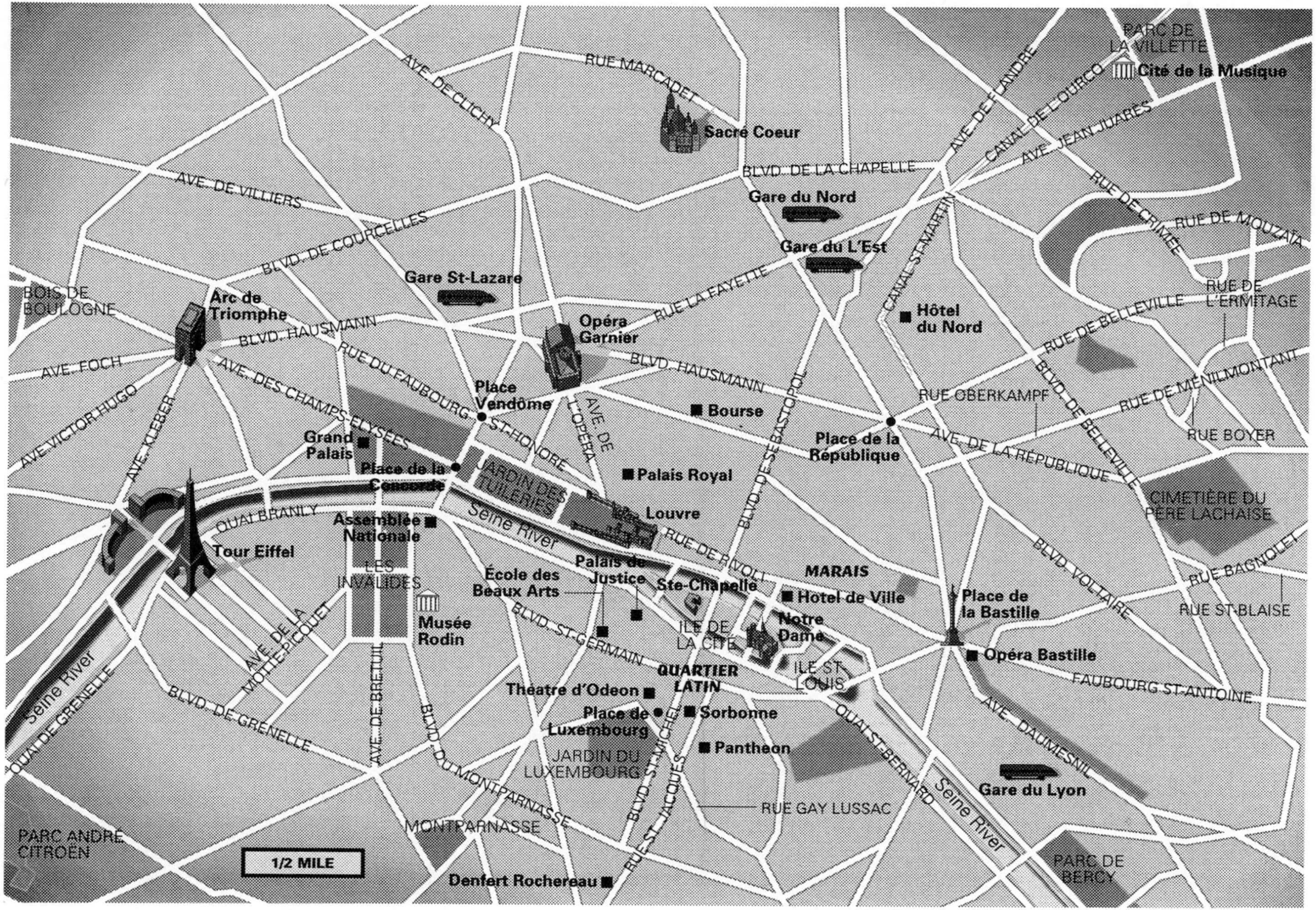

PARC DE LA VILLETTE
Cité de la Musique
RUE MARCADET
AVE. DE CLICHY
Sacré Coeur
BLVD. DE LA CHAPELLE
AVE. DE FLANDRE
CANAL DE L'OURCQ
AVE. JEAN JAURES
AVE. DE VILLIERS
Gare du Nord
RUE DE CRIMEE
RUE DE MOUZAIA
BLVD. DE COURCELLES
Gare du L'Est
Gare St-Lazare
BOIS DE BOULOGNE
Arc de Triomphe
RUE LA FAYETTE
CANAL ST-MARTIN
Hôtel du Nord
RUE DE L'ERMITAGE
RUE DE BELLEVILLE
BLVD. HAUSMANN
Opéra Garnier
AVE. FOCH
RUE DU FAUBOURG
AVE. DES CHAMPS-ELYSEES
Place Vendôme
ST-HONORE
AVE. DE L'OPÉRA
Bourse
RUE OBERKAMPF
BLVD. DE BELLEVILLE
RUE DE MÉNILMONTANT
AVE. VICTOR HUGO
AVE. KLEBER
Grand Palais
Place de la Concorde
JARDIN DES TUILERIES
Palais Royal
BLVD. DE SEBASTOPOL
Place de la République
AVE. DE LA RÉPUBLIQUE
RUE BOYER
Louvre
CIMETIÈRE DU PÈRE LACHAISE
QUAI BRANLY
Assemblée Nationale
Seine River
RUE DE RIVOLI
Tour Eiffel
LES INVALIDES
École des Beaux Arts
Palais de Justice
Ste-Chapelle
MARAIS
BLVD. VOLTAIRE
RUE BAGNOLET
Hotel de Ville
Place de la Bastille
RUE ST-BLAISE
Musée Rodin
BLVD. ST-GERMAIN
ILE DE LA CITÉ
Notre Dame
AVE. DE LA MOTTE-PICQUET
Opéra Bastille
ILE ST-LOUIS
QUARTIER LATIN
FAUBOURG ST-ANTOINE
Seine River
QUAI DE GRENELLE
BLVD. DE GRENELLE
Theatre d'Odeon
Place de Luxembourg
Sorbonne
AVE. DE BRETEUIL
BLVD. DU MONTPARNASSE
BLVD. ST-MICHEL
Pantheon
QUAI ST-BERNARD
AVE. DAUMESNIL
JARDIN DU LUXEMBOURG
Gare du Lyon
RUE GAY LUSSAC
Seine River
PARC ANDRÉ CITROËN
MONTPARNASSE
RUE ST. JACQUES
1/2 MILE
PARC DE BERCY
Denfert Rochereau

GRAFFITI FROM THE WALLS OF PARIS: 1968

It is forbidden to forbid. Freedom begins by forbidding something: interference with the freedom of others.

Run comrade, the old world is behind you.

The Revolution must take place in men before occurring in things.

The walls have ears. Your ears have walls.

The act institutes the consciousness.

To desire reality is good! To realize one's desires is better.

The thought of tomorrow's enjoyment will never console me for today's boredom.

A single nonrevolutionary weekend is infinitely bloodier than a month of permanent revolution.

Beneath the cobblestones is the beach.

We are all German Jews.

Be salted, not sugared.

I am in the service of no one, the people will serve themselves.

The barricade blocks the street but opens the way.

Art is dead, liberate our daily life.

Life is elsewhere.

The restraints imposed on pleasure excite the pleasure of living without restraints.

The more I make love, the more I want to make the Revolution, the more I make the Revolution, the more I want to make love.

All power to the imagination!

Poetry is in the street.

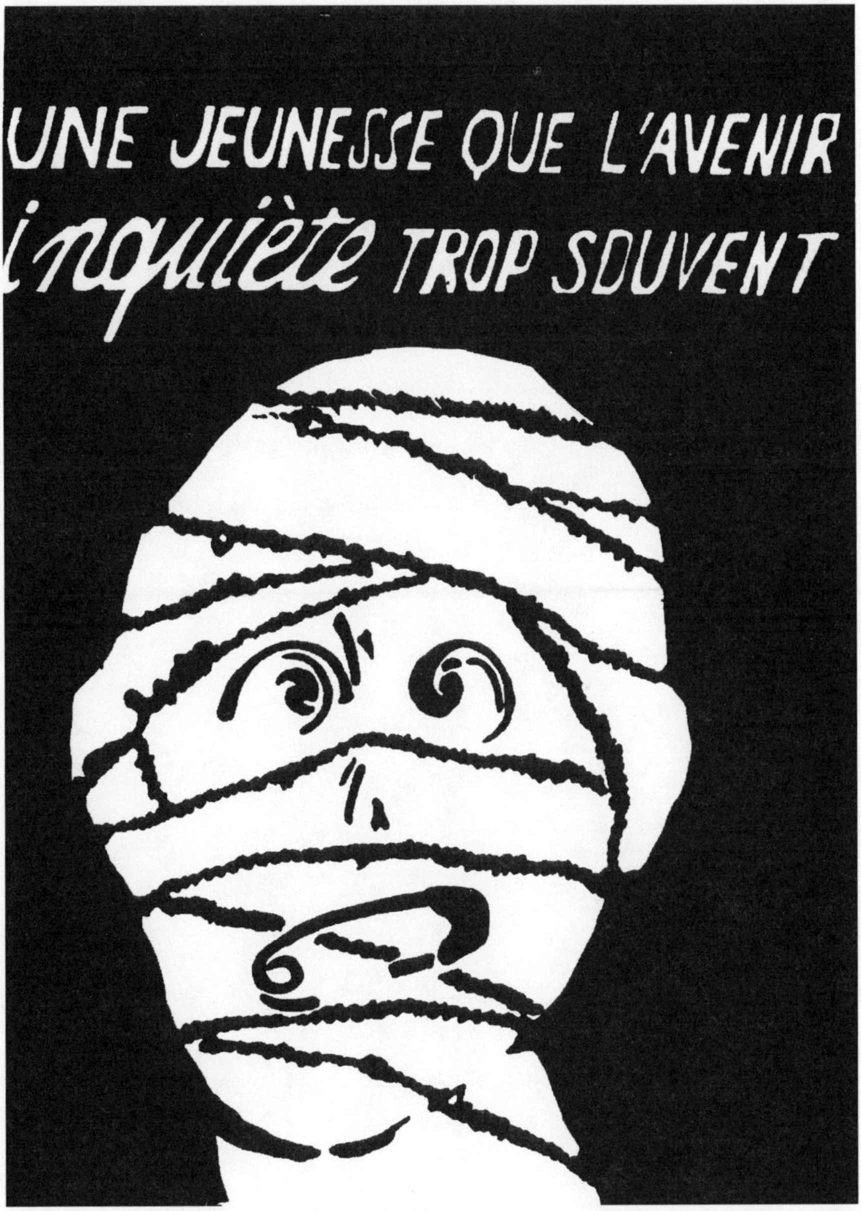
UNE JEUNESSE QUE L'AVENIR
inquiète TROP SOUVENT

CONTENTS

Contents

ILLUSTRATIONS

Cover Illustration: Mai 68 Début d'une Lutte Prolongé (May 68 Beginning of a Long-term Struggle)

Frontispiece: Students in front of the Renault factory at Boulogne-Billancourt in the south of Paris in 1968. Andrew Feenberg is visible in the background on the right reading a leaflet.

FOREWORD

May 1968 in France: Dynamics and Consequences

In the historical memory of the Left, the Events of May 1968 in France have attained mythic proportion. The student uprising, workers' strikes, and factory occupations that erupted during a brief but explosive period in 1968 instilled fear in the hearts of ruling powers everywhere. They inspired those in revolt everywhere with the faith that social upheaval is possible and that spontaneous insurgency can overcome the force of circumstances. For an all-too-brief moment, imagination seized power, the impossible was demanded, and poetry and spontaneity ruled the streets.

Of course, the revolutionary energies of the May Events were soon exhausted, order was restored, and since then the significance of May 1968 has been passionately debated. Did the uprising reveal the exhaustion and bankruptcy of the existing political system and parties, or the immaturity and undisciplined anarchy of the forces in revolt? Did the Events indicate the possibility of fundamental change, or prove that the established system can absorb all forms of opposition and contestation? Did May 1968 signal the autonomy of cultural and social revolution, or demonstrate once again that the old economic and political forces still control the system and can resist all change?

By now, a small library of books and articles have addressed the May Events and offered a myriad of conflicting interpretations. After a series of activities in 1998 commemorating the thirtieth anniversary of May 1968 and as a new millennium dawns, the Events themselves are buried in the historical archives, shrouded in dim remembrance, and mystified by clichéd media images and discourses. It is thus extremely useful to have access for the first time in English to many key original documents accompanied by a lucid and engaging record of the Events. Feenberg and Freedman have assembled a valuable collection of primary documents that provide a feeling for the immediacy and passion of the May Events, that disclose the explosion of radical thought it elicited, and that provide important evidence of the discourse and action of resistance in an advanced capitalist society. The documents reveal the self-understanding of the actual participants in the Events and allow them to speak directly to us, across the ages to a different historical conjuncture.

As participants and firsthand observers of the Events, Feenberg and Freedman provide a lively account that allows today's readers to grasp the chronology and significance of the explosion in France and experience the excitement and drama of what now appears as one of the most surprising and powerful contestations of the established political and economic system in the second half of the twentieth century. Their narrative is engaging and spirited, capturing the novelty and intensity of the Events, their complexity and contradictions, and the genuine excitement of what now appears as the last major revolutionary uprising in the Western world.

Feenberg and Freedman also provide lucid interpretive perspectives to make sense of the Events of May 1968, and challenge the current and coming generations of students and workers to renew radical contestation in the struggle for social transformation. Their assembled documents and analyses suggest to us today that resistance and action is feasible, that students and intellectuals can be harbingers of social transformation and agents of effective action, and that an oppressive system can be challenged and changed.

Feenberg and Freedman present the May Events in the first instance as a revolt against a technocratic system and as evidence that contestation and alternatives to this system are viable. Their documents and analyses show that middle-class students, intellectuals, and artists can organize themselves to transform their immediate places of work and everyday life and can unite with workers to militate for fundamental social transformation.

May 1968 demonstrates as well that spontaneous action can erupt quickly and surprisingly, that it can provide alternatives to standard politics, and that a new politics is practical and necessary. The initial inability of established Left political parties and unions to support the students and workers suggests the irrelevancy of politics as usual and the need to go outside of ordinary political channels and institutions to spark significant contestation and change. The Events also suggest the primacy of social and cultural revolution, of the need to change individuals, social relations, and culture as a prelude to political and systemic transformation. The total nature of the rebellion reflects the totalizing domination of the system that must itself be transformed if significant change is to take place.

Of course, the dispersion of revolutionary energy and aspirations, and the defeat of the more militant demands and forces, suggests as well that spontaneity is not enough, that passion and good ideas alone will not bring about change, and that the forms and organization of radical social change must be discovered. Feenberg and Freedman show that the radical student and worker cadres indeed put forward the concept of an alternative democratic organization of society and everyday life: self-management and the tradition of the workers' councils. Yet while autonomous, local organizing and struggle were defining features of the initial phase of the insurrection, and while demands for self-management and participation united students and workers in opposition, self-sustaining political organizations were never realized. Indeed, although the disparate groups came together in a General Strike that paralyzed French society and created conditions for genuinely revolutionary transformation, de Gaulle outmaneuvered the opposition and doomed it to defeat.

And yet people and social life were changed. I studied in France in 1971–1972 and almost all the young people I met told me with excitement of their participation in May 1968, swore that they would never conform or be "integrated" into the system, that the Events had changed their lives in significant ways. May 1968 was thus in retrospect a key event of the cultural revolution that was the 1960s, that most dramatically expressed the desire to break with established patterns of thought and behavior. May 1968 was an opening; it was a harbinger of a possible change that appeared to be in motion on a world-historical scale.

To properly understand the immediate force and lasting significance of the Events of May 1968 it should be stressed that the insurrection in France was part of what looked like a worldwide revolutionary movement, with branches in Latin America, China and Indochina, Japan, and Mexico. The May Events seemed to confirm that the system was under significant attack. The forces of contestation appeared to be gaining ascendancy on a world scale and would soon rupture the continuum of domination.

These hopes were dashed and a contradictory legacy of May 1968 emerged instead. As the assembled documents attest, for participants in the May Events, communist parties and the model of Soviet Marxism were shown to be completely bankrupt, part and parcel of the existing system of domination, and incapable of promoting genuine social and political revolution. It was necessary to cut revolutionary hopes free of those discredited experiments in the East. But for some, that break combined with the reinstallation of the Gaullist order in France and defeat of the revolutionary forces disclosed the bankruptcy of politics itself, suggesting that opposition and alternatives could only come from the margins of society, that only sustained micropolitics was viable.

Thus, in place of the revolutionary rupture in the historical continuum that 1968 had tried to produce, nascent postmodern theory in France postulated an epochal coupure, a break with modern politics and modernity, accompanied by models of new postmodern theory and politics. Hence, the postmodern turn in France in the 1970s is intimately connected to the experiences of May 1968. The passionate intensity and spirit of critique in many versions of French postmodern theory is a continuation of the spirit of 1968, while the world-weary nihilism of Baudrillard and some of his followers can be related to the defeat and dispiriting aftermath of the Events of May.

Indeed, Baudrillard, Lyotard, Virilio, Derrida, Castoriadis, Foucault, Deleuze, Guatarri, and other French theorists associated with postmodern theory were all participants in May 1968. They shared its revolutionary elan and radical aspirations, and they attempted to develop new modes of radical thought that carried on in a different historical conjuncture the radicalism of the 1960s. But whereas theorists like Herbert Marcuse and Henri Lefebrve found confirmation of their brand of utopian Marxism in the explosions of May, these postmodern theorists saw the need to break with all past forms of thought and politics and to create new ones.

For us today, May 1968 continues to raise fundamental problems. The documents, analysis, and interpretation set out in this book suggest the following challenges for contemporary advanced societies:

- Can a highly organized technological society offer fulfilling work to its members, or must they be reduced to cogs in the machine?
- Can bureaucracies and the workplace be reshaped to allow more freedom, initiative, participation, and non-alienating activity, or are we condemned to bureaucratic and technocratic domination?

- Can the citizens of contemporary societies recover the energy and initiative necessary for a democratic public life, or have they been permanently stifled by mindless work and entertainment?
- Does technological progress condemn us to live and work under the control of technocratic experts and smart machines, or can we find more democratic ways to deploy our technologies and organize our society?

These questions were posed with passionate intensity by the French students and workers, and the documents in this book challenge us also to consider how we want to work and live. Will we submit forever to alienating bureaucracies and workplace routines, or can we restructure the workplace and our social institutions? Will we allow ourselves to be governed by political elites and institutions that are unresponsive to people's needs and aspirations, or can we create a political system that is more participatory and democratic? Are we content to be passive consumers of culture and media spectacles, or can we create our own culture and make our own history?

For a brief moment, the spirit of 1968 appeared to promise fundamental change in France and other places throughout the world. To counter historical forgetting, to keep memory and hope alive let us now rethink and relive these experiences, find connections with our contemporary situation, and strive to create our own alternative modes of thought and action. Andrew Feenberg and Jim Freedman are to be thanked for their work in assembling documents that allow us to gain access to an exciting historical occurrence. Now it is up to us and the coming generations to draw the appropriate conclusions.

—Douglas Kellner

PREFACE

Nineteen sixty-eight was the climactic year of New Left protest all over the Western world, and especially in France where in May of that year ten million workers transformed a student protest into a revolutionary movement by joining it in the streets. In the short space of a month France was overthrown and restored, but not without suffering a shock that resounds to this day. Like many an unsuccessful revolution before it, the May Events triumphed in the political culture of the society that defeated it in the streets. Although the Events occurred in France, they reveal many of the underlying causes of student protest throughout the advanced capitalist world, including the United States.

The May Events lay at the intersection of three histories: not only did the New Left of the sixties peak in France in 1968, but France gave the first signal of the political instability that overtook much of Southern Europe in the seventies. In 1968 no one imagined that the Events would lead to an electoral movement such as Eurocommunism. Then the talk was all of the "senility" and "sclerosis" of the official opposition parties. In fact, the May Events overthrew not the Gaullist state, but the narrow ideological horizons of the Old Left it challenged in challenging capitalism in new ways. The Events transformed the popular image of socialism in France, contributing to the collapse of moribund Stalinist and social democratic traditions, and prepared Mitterand's eventual victory as the first "socialist" president of the Fifth Republic.

However, that victory failed to yield radical social change. The Socialist and Communist parties had flirted with the energies and ideas circulating in the extraparliamentary Left since 1968, but in the end abandoned their flirtation for a banal program of nationalizations followed by a hasty retreat into fiscal and political conservatism. Thus what remained of the influence of the Events was once again an extra-

and even antiparliamentary opposition left to its own devices. In this alienating situation the new social movements, such as the environmental and feminist movements, were finally able to come out from under the shadow of the established Left parties. Meanwhile, French intellectuals were also liberated from the moral burden of communist ideology that had weighed on them since World War II. New theoretical movements associated with the names of Foucault, Deleuze, and Baudrillard finished the break with the Old Left begun in 1968.

The May Events were at once the last gasp of the old socialist tradition and the first signal of a new kind of opposition. They are important to us today as a link with the past and as harbingers of the politics of the future. This book presents the Events from three different angles. We include a narrative that recounts the causes and unfolding of the struggles, the rise and fall of the movement. Without this historical background, the significance of the Events cannot be grasped. There follow four groups of translated documents, mainly leaflets distributed during the Events and short articles describing typical struggles or movements. These texts offer insight into the thinking and experiences of a wide range of participants. We have arranged the translations according to the main themes of the movement. Each of these four groups of doments is prefaced by an essay, written by Andrew Feenberg, which explains the translated texts and relates them to the history and theory of revolution.

We would like to thank Garrick Davis for help in the preparation of the manuscript, and for suggesting the (very poetic) title of this book.

ABBREVIATIONS

CAL	High School Action Committee
CARS	Revolutionary Action Committee of the Sorbonne
CDR	Committee for Republican Defense, a right wing organization
CERAU	Study and Research Center for Urban Development
CFDT	French Democratic Confederation of Labor, France's second largest labor union
CGC	General Confederation of Cadres (executives)
CGT	General Confederation of Workers, France's largest labor union, including the General Union of Civil Servants
CLEOP	Puteaux Inter-Union Council
CNRS	National Center for Scientific Research
CNSA	Union of Agriculturalists
CRAC	Revolutionary Committee for Cultural Agitation
CRS	Security Police Force
EDF	Electricity Utility of France
ENSEA	National Union of Entrepreneurial Farmers
FER	Federation of Revolutionary Students
FO	Workers' Force
INSEE	National Institute for Statistics
JCR	Young Communist Revolutionaries
MNEF	National Movement of French Students, one of two student unions
PCF	French Communist Party
SNCF	France's National Railway Company
SNEsup	National Union of Professors of Higher Education
UEC	Union of Communist Students

Abbreviations

UJCML   Union of Marxist-Leninist Communist Youth

UNEF   National Union of French Students, one of two student unions

ONE

WHAT HAPPENED IN MAY: A CHRONICLE

Andrew Feenberg and Jim Freedman

PART I. STUDENTS VERSUS SOCIETY

La Phase Nanterroise

What was most surprising about the revolutionary movement that swept an apparently placid and comfortable France in May 1968 was its rapidity and short duration. It started at the University of Nanterre, where a small kernel of twenty-five grew into over a thousand in a month's time, sufficient to arrest the university's normal functioning. A week after the closing of Nanterre, the group of radicals swelled to fifty thousand and, in another ten days, ten million. In another month, like a comet, it had disappeared; except for some raises in salaries, minor changes in de Gaulle's cabinet, and specks of unwashed graffiti on the walls of the Sorbonne, there was hardly a visible trace of its passing.

How to interpret these events that fit only awkwardly into the annals of history? Should the movement be recognized as a close-but-not-quite fulfillment of the Marxist malediction of capitalist society? Or is the reverse true—that the eventual failure of the movement and de Gaulle's subsequent electoral success is final proof that consumer capitalism and private enterprise will live forever?

It is especially astounding that the movement, which begs by its Marxist, Maoist, and Marcusean inspiration for a socialist explanation, should have started at Nanterre. For this city was a suburban outpost of bourgeois family life, full of young people whose future was staked in the success of capitalism, arch-consumers of a consumer culture.[1] That there arose in such a place, within a few weeks' time, a revolt that shook France to her industrial roots, that made de Gaulle brandish the threat of civil war, that closed every school, paralyzed hundreds of factories and changed forever the politics of the nation, puts historical credibility to the test.

---

1. The words "bourgeois" and "proletarian" will recur often in this book. These terms refer, of course, to the upper and working classes of a capitalist society. Although they are hardly used in contemporary American speech anymore, they were commonplace terms in France in 1968, especially on the left, that is to say, among the nearly 50 percent of the population which voted for the Communist and socialist parties.

Before addressing the larger question of the meaning of the Events, the historian must pose more specific ones such as: Why did the movement begin at Nanterre? What is the mystery of this suburban revolt? Why weren't the workers first to the barricades? Their lot had changed little since their last major uprising in 1936, despite the increasing prosperity of France. An answer, but by no means the answer, lies somewhere in a combination of three phenomena that converged on the University of Nanterre in the year 1968.[2]

First of all there was the *phénomène Nanterre* itself, its physical aspect. Ten miles west of Paris, where pastel colors take on an industrial brown, the cobblestone streets and delicate architecture of the city are replaced by urban industry and dingy housing projects. Pasted onto this landscape, on the site of an old army campground surrounded by a high gray stone wall is a complex of buildings, the University of Nanterre, practically indistinguishable from its fellow factories of fresh cement and steel.

Nanterre was a far cry from the Sorbonne where students' lives were unquestionably their own, where they frequented cafés and friends unimpeded in every respect. At Nanterre, with nothing else to do, the students were obliged to stay and attend classes, which meant that they were just about the only permanent residents; professors came seldom and only for courses, ironically because they wanted little to do with the unattractive life of Nanterre and its cloistered students.

The paradox haunted Nanterre for a further reason. The university had been built in a spirit of reform, as a proving ground for experiments in student participation in university governance. The administration was authorized to give wide rein to student expression, letting the campus develop much as its constituent body willed. A young faculty attempted in various ways to reduce the distance that traditionally separated students from professors, and courses from modern life. But even though students and faculty were encouraged to experiment, the immense glacier of French educational bureaucracy ground down their efforts, and no real reforms were ever accepted.

Such was the phenomenon of Nanterre: a student body frustrated by its surroundings, experiencing diffused and undirected discontent, given a sense of its importance, but denied a real voice.

Nanterre's second grave problem was the Fouchet Reforms of

---

2. In 1936 a socialist "Popular Front" government was elected. A general strike soon pushed it to the left, and it granted wage increases and instituted major reforms.

French higher education. These reforms were a timid Americanization of the French system—a little more competition, a little less leisure time for exploring what lay beyond the pedagogic mysteries. Generally, the reforms were an encroachment on the free spirit for the sake of efficiency. For instance: laboratory discussion sessions, given in conjunction with large lecture courses, heretofore optional were now required; students had to choose their specialty in the first year of higher education, and, should they fail one year, they were allotted only a single extra year to make it up before being dropped.

The reformers were interested in efficiency. French youth, however, were sensitive to the delicate balance between individuality and culture. Required courses, required attendance, a limited number of years to complete the educational process—all appeared to sacrifice the leisure of learning embedded in French tradition and raised the dreaded specter of a monolithic society.

The day of reckoning for the Fouchet Reforms came on November 10, 1967, when the entire program, despite numerous appeals from professors to apply the reform progressively, was "parachuted" onto the French system. At Nanterre, it simply did not make it through the already sensitized atmosphere. A minority of students refused to attend classes until assured of some revision of the reforms. Only after a group of professors negotiated some concessions with the Ministry did courses resume normally.

These November boycotts left their mark on Nanterre, awakening dormant discontents and bringing a normally apathetic student body into an active relationship with the university and the society. The resultant student agitation was the third factor threatening the order of things at Nanterre.

After November, two groups of activists were distinguishable. On the one hand were those who set about to reform the Fouchet Reforms. From them came the idea of Paritary Commissions—committees of students and professors set up in each department to solve problems related to course schedules, grievances, and the lack of communication between the administration and the student body. It was a fine idea, the most legitimate solution to the university problem, but it was not taken seriously by the Ministry. On the other hand were students who were already politically mature radicals. Among them, the most spectacular were the notorious *enragés,* who rejected the Fouchet Reforms outright.[3]

---

3. "*Enragés*" are literally angry. As the name of a political group, the term derives from the French Revolution of 1789.

They saw the university, and particularly Nanterre, as the Golden Calf of an inhuman government that itself deserved to be destroyed.

These few *enragés* created an alternative solution at Nanterre—one might say an alternative to Nanterre. Flaunting all custom, respecting nothing, breaking up lecture courses in the name of Mao Tse-Tung and Che Guevera, they created a continual political happening. Their basic goals were, first, to leave the authorities no peace; second, to convey the idea that the ills of students were attributable not to the structure of the university, but to the structure of society, and that denunciation and possibly even revolution were the only reasonable means of protest. None of this won them any popularity votes, at the most a few chuckles for their antics, but they did succeed in creating an awareness of political issues among the student population.

Early in 1968 the *enragés* passed from theoretical debates to direct action against the authorities. They had their opportunity following a fortuitous incident on January 26. On this day, the *enragés* were on parade, all forty of them, marching down the long Nanterre corridor when the rumor started that an opposition political group of right-wing militants called *Occident* planned a counterdemonstration. "Counterdemonstration," in this context, could only be a euphemism for a fight. Someone called the police who, on arriving, began to disperse the students with clubs and tear gas. In the closed arena that was Nanterre a crowd soon gathered, angered simply by the presence of law officers in the university; much to the surprise of the police, this amorphous crowd of bystanders returned their blows with rocks and improvised weapons. This was the beginning of the Nanterre mobilization. Little matter how it started, the presence of police in the university was an irreparable offense.

With a little luck, the *enragés* had exposed Nanterre's isolated community to the most unpopular form of authority: physical repression. This produced a visible justification for total opposition to the university. Here was a confirmation of many students' objections to the Fouchet Reforms: the very same government that had conceived of these reforms could bring police onto university grounds in violation of the traditional immunity of the university.[4] A second police invasion followed the January 26 incident; this one took place progressively as a

---

4. Since the Middle Ages, French universities have enjoyed a kind of semi-independence from the local authorities. Police on campus was inconceivable to the generation of students and teachers active in 1968.

fifth column of civilian policemen slowly established itself in the classes and halls of Nanterre. These undercover cops had a blacklist of "undesirables" in which the *enragés* professed an honor to be inscribed. What all this meant was that the control was slowly slipping from the grasp of Dean Grappin, the liberal head of the university, and into that of a sinister police crew.

Police in the university dramatized the conflict between state repression and student freedom, and served as proof of the validity of protest.[5] From that point on, a growing number of newly *enragés* swelled meetings in which topics of discussion varied from police brutality to Vietnam to freedom of expression. No organization determined policy; everyone spoke as inspired, and no adherence to a doctrine was required. In contrast to other political organizations on campus, an *enragé* felt no obligation or political commitment, had no card to carry, no register to sign, and this spontaneity in itself added to the group's ambiguous popularity.

The *enragés* learned and conveyed the following lesson: tactical agitation is the Achilles heel of a rigid administration. Conspicuous disturbance frustrates authority, which in turn increases restrictive measures, which in turn more fully justify protest. Once caught in this escalation of protest and repression the administration is bound to lose, whether it capitulates or suppresses its opposition. By early March, the process was well under way. More agitation led to more police, which in turn further poisoned the atmosphere at Nanterre. Meetings now overflowed the capacity of their assigned room, yet Dean Grappin refused to grant another larger room, hoping that if he could not dissuade he could at least squeeze out his opposition. His response only gave the *enragés* another platform for protest. Similarly, in mid-March, Grappin refused to ask for the release of four demonstrators, arrested during a Vietnam protest march at the Paris American Express Office. The four demonstrators became martyrs, and tempers flared.

The escalation of tempers and tension reached a high point on March 22 when five hundred students joined the *enragés* in a meeting and spontaneously decided to take decisive action. Toward evening, a hundred and forty-two members entered the sacred faculty conference room on the eighth floor of a central campus building and occupied it during the entire night, protesting in the name of freedom of expression

---

5. For a history of the movement at Nanterre, see A. F. Gaussen's "L'Université entre deux ages, II," *Le Monde,* 8 Mai 1968, p. 7.

and their four arrested comrades. There, on this memorable night, they gave birth and baptism to a new movement. It was incongruous but true that the history of Nanterre and possibly France would hinge on the agitation of so small a group, who called themselves the March 22 Movement from that moment on.

The movement, born in this act of opposition and committed to revolution, created new problems for the administration again and again. They won a major round when Grappin granted them the largest hall in the university, and soon this too held a capacity audience. During succeeding days, meeting followed meeting and their ranks swelled to a thousand. They announced the boycott of midterm exams, to which Dean Grappin replied by closing the university. On the reopening and rescheduling of exams, the March 22 Movement scored a major victory when three hundred students responded to the boycott. Following Easter vacation the movement planned a two-week conference entitled "Anti-imperialist Days," including a series of talks on subjects ranging from Vietnam to student struggles in underdeveloped countries.

On April 17 at Nanterre, Dr. Laurent Schwartz, one of the world's most famous physicists, came to speak on the Fouchet Reforms. Chaos reigned in the hall and some students shouted that an anti-revolutionary should not be allowed to speak.

Daniel Cohn-Bendit, redheaded, elastic, and jovial, rose above the confusion without a microphone; when he motioned to be heard, silence was reestablished. "Laurent Schwartz should be allowed to explain himself" he shouted. "Let him speak and afterwards, if we think he is rotten, we will say, 'Monsieur Laurent Schwartz, you are rotten.'" And for the moment, order was restored and everyone got down from the stage.[6] There was no chairperson. Cohn-Bendit refused to impose any authority, so every orator had to express himself and be criticized amid the chaos.

Cohn-Bendit was the symbol and the anti-symbol of the movement. He was the leader, but denied the concept of leadership; he had originated the March 22 Movement, but claimed that the presence of an organization could only work to the detriment of revolt. Although he disclaimed such a thing as a "cult of personality," the spontaneity that was the sense of the movement and the reason for its incredible success was incarnate in him.

A student returning to Nanterre by chance on April 17 after a two-

---

6. A. F. Gaussen and Guy Herzlich, "Le Rêve de Nanterre," *Le Monde,* 7 Mai 1968, p. 1.

or three-year absence would have been much surprised. Student political action, particularly since the Algerian war ended in 1962, had worn down to a very low ebb. Foundering in factions, it was an arena of despair, of small, ineffective, squabbling organizations. Cohn-Bendit introduced two major new directions. First, he created a movement that was flexible, in which every political theory could find a place. Second, he wished to unite those holding these various positions in spontaneously inspired direct action. With such a strategy, temporary goals could be proposed, then rendered concrete and acceptable to a broad range of political orientations.

This was something that established political organizations had not been able to do. The only one that had come close was UNEF, the National Union of French Students, which, up to 1963 had held sway among the students. UNEF reached the pinnacle of its influence during the Algerian War when it took a strong stand for Algerian Independence. Its numbers at that time rose to a record high of 100,000. However, following the Algerian crisis, the government (which had previously funded UNEF) withdrew its support. At the same time, student political consciousness decreased considerably, leaving the once central organization with neither political nor monetary substance. Its assemblies became tumultuous circuses of diverse splinter groups, its chapters mostly reduced to small gatherings of desperadoes.

The United States unwittingly changed all this. Its war in Vietnam inspired fresh protest on which there could be wide accord and an extension of activism beyond the university and even beyond France into concern with the ills of imperialism. The March 22 Movement belittled all reforms within the confines of the university, instead advocating direct action to change society. By venturing into the factories that conveniently surrounded Nanterre, talking with workers, and rallying support for greater wage demands, they made a critical point: it was not only the university that was at fault but the entire society.

One of the most outstanding aspects of the movement was its vocal anti-communism. The communists' handicap was similar, in a sense, to that of UNEF: institutionalized protest was not wanted. Ironically, the party's greatest problem at Nanterre in April was at the same time its strongest asset in France—that it was respectable. "We are all undesirable," the famous declaration of Cohn-Bendit, was repugnant to the communist conception of the propriety of protest.

Hardly suspecting that the March 22 Movement would launch a nationwide revolt from the meager beginnings of a dozen anarchists, the party kept its distance. The party was still abusing them on May 3, after Nanterre was closed for the second and last time and after the first major confrontation between students and police. "These false revolutionaries," the party organ *Humanité* reported, "ought to be unmasked, because, in fact, they serve the interests of the Gaullist state. . . . It is necessary to combat and completely isolate the extreme leftist *'groupuscules'* who want only to harm the democratic process by drowning it in talk."[7]

Like the Communist Party, almost no one took the movement seriously. By its radicalism and its total refusal of any normal order, it seemed to be situated in cloud-cuckoo land, hardly in the reality of national politics. The major unions distributed leaflets in the factories warning workers against young subversives. In fact, as one observer noted, they seemed to live a kind of collective dream, carried away by a movement feeding on its own growth.

May 2 was another spring day at Nanterre, but this one surpassed in disorder even the turmoil and unrest that had become normal there; this day was particularly noteworthy for it marked the end of the *phase nanterroise*. The morning proceeded in an abnormally burlesque fashion: Dean Grappin denied the students' request to use the loudspeaker system, so they entered his office and seized it. Grappin locked them inside the office, but the students exited through an open window. The March 22 Movement then occupied a lecture hall, refusing a history professor his class time, while engineers installed the loudspeaker system and the occupants struck up a verse of the *Internationale*.

In an already strained atmosphere, the day was further marked by an announcement that Cohn-Bendit had been called to appear before a disciplinary council in Paris on Monday. Classes were impossible where disorder reigned. Dean Grappin called the Minister of Education, Alain Peyrefitte, to request permission to close the university for the second time in a month—this time indefinitely. The next time Nanterre would open, it would be a "free and autonomous university" in the service of the revolution.

---

7. George Marchais, *L'Humanité*, 3 Mai 1968, p. 10. *Groupuscules* was the derisive name given to the many small political sects on the Left. It would be tedious to describe them all. Most were either Trotskyist, representing various revolutionary Marxist positions critical of the Soviet Union and the French Communist Party, or Maoist, advocating a Chinese-style revolution for France, and also critical of the Soviet Union and the French Communist Party. The Trotskyist movements still exist and have a certain national visibility, if not much support.

Friday Red I

May 3, first of the famous Fridays, found Nanterre's militants crowding into the Sorbonne's courtyard where, under the auspices of UNEF, a meeting had been called to explain the closing of Nanterre the day before. As classes concluded, around 1:00 P.M., the courtyard began to fill up. Cohn-Bendit was there, carrying a megaphone, as was his custom.

Parallel to the emergence of Nanterre's boisterous radicalism in past months, a militant right-wing organization known as *Occident* experienced a revival of its own brand of political activity that consisted, in short, of terrorizing left-wing organizations. Its members prided themselves on being the independent "toughs" in defense of freedom and order, and in the *enragés* they found a perfect target for their so-called political program.

The menace of *Occident* had come to weigh more and more heavily on all leftist political activity. For this reason, on Friday afternoon, as a few members of *Occident* lingered several blocks away on the Boulevard St. Michel, the organizers of the Sorbonne meeting took precautions. As had been common practice in almost every meeting during the last few weeks, the organizers appointed student monitors, provided them with motorcycle helmets and chair legs, and designated them to keep on the lookout. In the Sorbonne, Cohn-Bendit appealed to the students not to capitulate in the face of the closing of Nanterre but to renew their attack on France's technocratic universities.

Another member announced amid great applause that Paris had been chosen as the host of peace talks between Vietnam and the United States. A representative from UNEF concluded the meeting by calling a gathering in front of the Sorbonne Monday morning to protest the required appearance before a disciplinary council of Cohn-Bendit and seven comrades from Nanterre. The meeting had begun and ended peacefully, but there was one false note: police protection against a rather dubious *Occident* attack had become surprisingly energetic, so that by 4:00 P.M. police vans completely surrounded the Sorbonne.

At this moment, someone came running into the courtyard shouting, "They are coming!" Who was coming? Against such magnificent protection, *Occident* didn't have a chance. For a moment, a flurry of curiosity ran through the crowd. In another instant, however, all questions were resolved. Standing against the back wall of the courtyard was a line of policemen, fitted out to provoke with helmets and clubs,

11

ordering the students to leave. This presented a peculiar contradiction since the main gate had been closed and other exits were blocked. Finally an officer opened the main gate, graciously permitting everyone to go, but as soon as the students passed through the door they were led straight away into paddy wagons.

The students felt themselves dupes of an administration ploy. Shortly, groups from the meeting joined by a number of others who had come to attend 5 o'clock classes, surrounded police cars filled with their friends incongruously peering from behind paddy wagon bars, and demanded to know how protection had become repression. A thousand students gathered during the bizarre process of assembly-line arrests and spontaneously decided to resist in some fashion. In the confusion that reigned in the streets outside the Sorbonne, no one knew for sure the exact moment when nonviolence passed into violence, but the arrests provoked an indignation that would mobilize massive defiance against the university, the police, and de Gaulle during the next week.

The clues to this revolt lie in interministerial phone conversations, clues that answer the all-important question of how police got into the courtyard of the Sorbonne in the first place. It seems that Rector Roche of the Sorbonne, fearing a destructive encounter between rival political groups, called Alain Peyrefitte—the Minister of Education. Peyrefitte had apparently been reluctant to intervene, though he agreed that Roche might speak with the Chief of Police. The Chief also had his reservations about sending police into the university, though finally he agreed to do so if the request was submitted in writing.[8] Roche then dashed off a letter and the train of powder was ignited.

As for the students, their response (and of this there is no doubt) was spontaneous. The invasion was for them a complete surprise; no one could have predicted it. Vague rumors (which were, in the end, untrue) of an attack by *Occident* had inspired the students to take some minor precautions against possible harassment. No one ever imagined an alliance between the university officials and the police to repress a political meeting. Understandably, students fought back.

"A few troublemakers," remarked Peyrefitte, in shoving the issue aside.[9] It was clearly not a question, however, of a few troublemakers or even a few Maoist mercenaries as Prime Minister Pompidou implied the following week. The movement was popular and undirected. A

---

8. B. Giron de l'Ain, "Un Manque de sang-froid," *Le Monde,* 6 Mai 1968, p. 9.
9. Ibid., p. 1.

week later, Cohn-Bendit offered a pertinent hindsight after seeing what May 3 and the first Red Friday had started: "No one can point to any person or leader as responsible. How can this be? It is the system which is violent. Of course we have resisted government power; after all it is this power which has sent its police against us. But we, the leaders, never considered sending the students into the streets because they would never have followed us."[10]

Sometime during the fighting, Rector Roche ordered the Sorbonne closed for the first time in history. (And it has a long history, going back to the Middle Ages.) The day ended in a telling paradox: its chief administrator had, in the literal sense of the term, turned the university inside out, flushing its students and professors into the streets in the name of an order that was only questionably threatened. The irony was complete but the revolution had only begun.

The Concept of Cobblestones

Back-to-back, on consecutive days, Dean Grappin and Rector Roche had closed their respective schools. They no doubt figured the odds were in their favor, reasoning that the number of students who incited the protest were few and would remain few, and that the imminent examinations would weigh so heavily on the majority of students that they would demand the early resumption of courses. On both counts they were grossly mistaken. The closing of the universities did not dampen the activists' passion, but justified it. It simply added another and stronger argument against an oppressive, paternalistic system, propelling them into the streets and across their Rubicon.

Friday night had counted a serious toll: six hundred students arrested, of whom twenty-eight were held for questioning, including Cohn-Bendit and Jacques Sauvageot, vice president and acting director of the National French Student Union (UNEF). Despite the fact that the Ministry of Interior and Chief of Police had forbidden all further demonstrations, the leaders of UNEF decided to launch an appeal for every student in Paris to meet for a demonstration in front of the Sorbonne, 9:00 Monday morning. The National Union of Professors of Higher Education (SNEsup) called a nationwide strike, beginning Monday, to demonstrate professors' sympathy with the students.

---

10. D. Cohn-Bendit, "Notre Commune de 10 Mai," *Le Nouvel Observateur,* no. 183, 15–21 Mai 1968, p. 33.

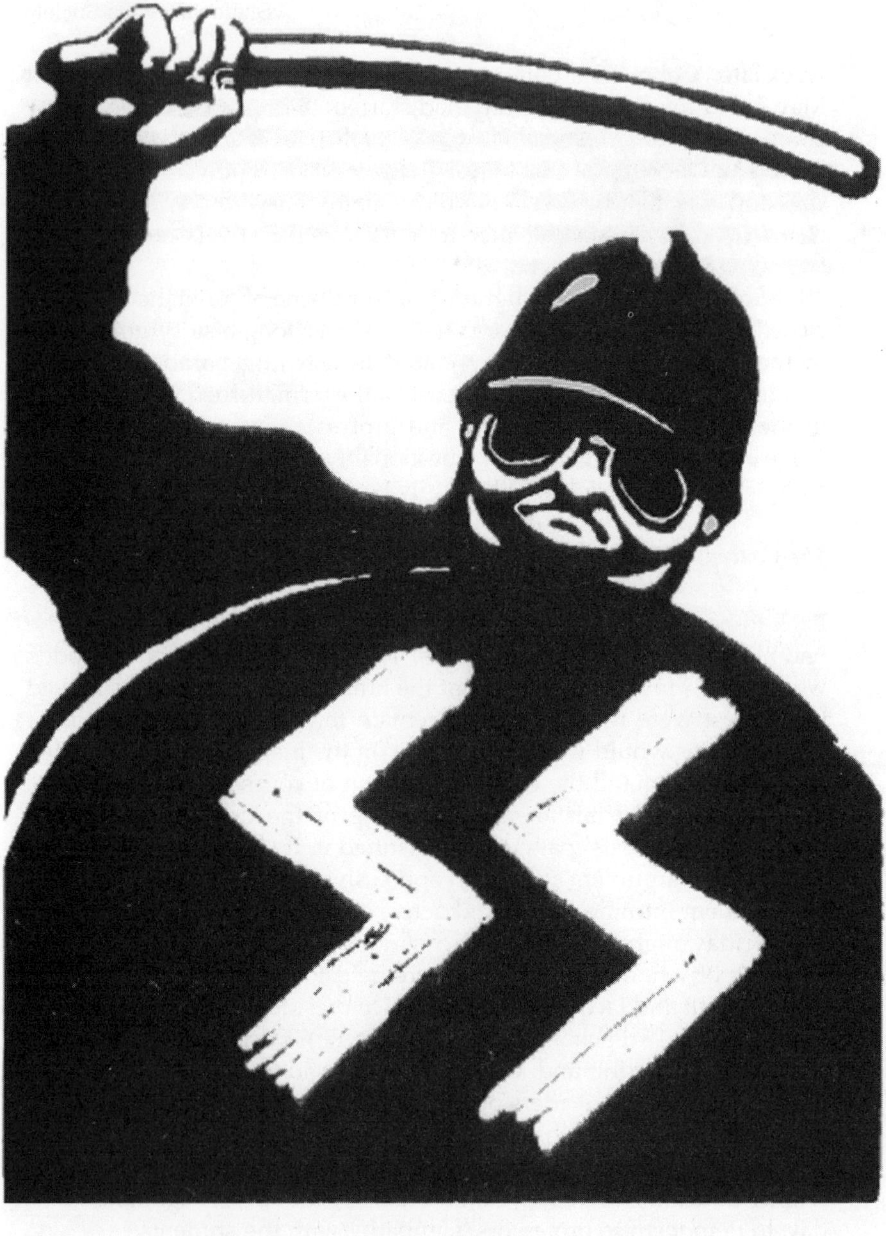

The March 22 Movement remained the acknowledged initiator and theoretical inspiration of the emerging mass movement, while its administrative leadership had by Monday morning been assumed by UNEF, which already had an established network of communications and contacts. While Cohn-Bendit remained the agitator, Jacques Sauvageot of UNEF became the spokesman. Alain Geismar, Secretary General of SNEsup, completed the triangle of leadership by which the movement identified itself in the coming week. Their policy was to accept no dialogue or appeasement before satisfaction of three conditions: release of their comrades detained during the events, reopening of the Sorbonne and Nanterre, and withdrawal of the police from the Latin Quarter.

The scene was set for Monday morning when the dawn came up on a massive troop of riot squad police, the *Comité Républicaine de Securité* (CRS), heavily armed with helmets, tear gas, clubs, and rifles. Cohn-Bendit with his seven companions from Nanterre made his way through a crowd of a thousand students who had gathered to support him, toward the Sorbonne and the disciplinary council. His style, not cramped in the slightest, was to walk jauntily, grinning with his companions, who were all singing the *Internationale*. They disappeared into a hedge of police.

The government had prohibited all demonstrations in order to preserve public order, but the prohibition had the reverse effect. A squadron of police, staked out at the base of St. Michel, where the boulevard intersects the river, charged an incipient demonstration and the first haze of tear gas hovered over the day. The escalation had begun. Following the police assault, lines formed and began to march away from the Sorbonne. Shortly, their numbers increased to five thousand as they made a tour of the Latin Quarter, crossing the Seine onto the right bank and back to the left bank by early afternoon, arriving finally at the Sorbonne where they met a major squadron of police head-on.

As the demonstration ascended Rue St. Jacques, just behind the Sorbonne, the CRS launched a brutal attack. The retreat left behind twenty bodies sprawled in the clear space. Before the police regained their position, unexpectedly, students assailed them with improvised weapons. Automobiles were strewn across the streets—blockades and barricades of diverse sorts sprung up. These momentary fortresses briefly warded off a second attack of tear gas, and the students moved backward along the wide Boulevard St. Germain. Repeated CRS charges failed to discourage the daring demonstrators, who eventually succeeded in creating an impenetrable bastion surrounded by fires, overturned cars, felled trees, and piles of cobblestones. Inevitably, however, the demonstrators were surrounded. Driven by the necessity of the moment and the impossibility of retreat, they divided up urgent duties: some turned up stones in the street, others formed lines to pass stones to needed locations, others ventured through the tear gas and debris, pitching their improvised missiles.

A scattering of demonstrators rallied again at 6:00 P.M., joined now by four of France's most eminent professors. Soon the crowd reached ten thousand, and marched once again toward the Sorbonne in a desperate attempt to pass the police. A new battle raged near the St. Germain-des-Prés subway station where the violence surpassed anything seen before, the surging masses in combat forming a bizarre sight amid the chic boutiques and cafés of the Parisian elite. The crowd never reached the Sorbonne, but fighting continued until dawn, sparse and mostly desperate skirmishes. Official reports recorded the astounding figures of Monday's debacle: six hundred wounded demonstrators, three hundred forty-five wounded policemen. Residents of the Latin Quarter gathered in the streets until late at night, despite the wreckage and the almost impenetrable haze of tear gas, shocked and dismayed by the brutality of the police that they had witnessed from their windows.

The Long Trek and a Short Truce

Le Monde reported Tuesday afternoon: "Paris experienced, Monday, the largest and most serious student demonstration in the last ten years. Even at the time of the Algerian War, there were no riots of this size and particularly of such duration."[11] *France Soir,* another Paris paper, asked, "How had it come to this?" It was a question everyone wanted answered.

But the government maintained a peculiar indifference. For Peyrefitte, what had happened was the regrettable but inevitable culmination of six months of agitation by political groups in the universities. He made no mention of student demands, little mention even of university reform, just a reprimand and an offer of dialogue.

After meetings of the UNEF and SNEsup Tuesday morning, Jacques Sauvageot conveyed the response of these organizations: "Dialogue is impossible between those who strike blows and those who are struck." They reaffirmed their order for a student boycott and a

---

11. "Les Manifestations de Lundi," *Le Monde,* 8 Mai 1968, p. 11.

strike by professors. They would cease their movement only when the authorities accepted their oft-repeated demands: release of arrested students with dismissal of all charges, withdrawal of police from the universities, and reopening of the two universities. UNEF called another demonstration for Tuesday evening.

A first attempt at appeasement came from sympathetic professors. Among them, as among the students, there were all sorts; it would be a mistake to assume them homogeneously in favor of the movement, though for the first time since the Algerian War, a significant number of them joined student demonstrations. On Tuesday morning they made two attempts to intervene, not necessarily in favor of the students, but for the prevention of violence. One of these consisted of a committee of seven professors who found themselves flatly refused an audience by Rector Roche. The other, a committee composed of Professors Jacob, Kastler, Lwoff, Mauriac, and Monod, all Nobel prize recipients, sent a telegram to General de Gaulle reiterating the demands of the students. No answer was forthcoming, either from de Gaulle or the Minister of the Interior.

A second sign of alarm, if not an attempt at appeasement, came from the Chief of Police, Grimaud, who was discreetly concerned about the escalation of fighting with the students. The chief sensed that the police invasion of the Sorbonne on Friday, a project that had never really appealed to him, had produced unfortunate results. This he publicly recognized, while at the same time he confirmed the prohibition of the upcoming UNEF march. The war with the police was now cold, but by no means abandoned. A modus vivendi was now agreed on—the demonstration would be permitted if the students stayed away from the Sorbonne.

Tuesday's march accomplished its purpose. As it approached the Seine, the original twenty-five thousand increased until, stopped at the river by a dam of police, their number reached approximately forty thousand. Then, quickly shifting direction, the marchers sidestepped police by heading for an unexpected bridge, and arrived at the Champs Elysée, where they showed the right bank of Paris the extent of their determination. Marching up the Champs Elysée to the Arc de Triomphe, singing the *Internationale,* they waved the red flag of communism and the black flag of anarchism. Finally, they headed back to the Latin Quarter. Once there, Sauvageot announced that they would try to reach the Sorbonne. Thirty kilometers of marching, however, had taken the fight out of most of them; shortly after crossing to the left bank, Sauvageot gave an order for dispersion.

Only a few remained to harass the police during the night, but their demonstration could not be ignored. They had surrounded France's sacred Unknown Soldier's Tomb with their motley revolution, singing the communist anthem under the Arc de Triomphe and publicly displaying their contempt for society's wealth on the jeweled Champs Elysée.

A new hope flourished among the students, that perhaps the literature of the streets: *LIBEREZ NOS CAMARADES, OUVREZ LA SORBONNE, LA SORBONNE AUX ETUDIANTS,* had not been written entirely in the air. The Council of Ministers, becoming more and more convinced of the breadth of the movement, admitted for the first time an extraordinary climate of unrest. Tuesday's long march and truce were proof again that Peyrefitte's first reaction, "a handful of troublemakers," was more wishful thinking than serious analysis.

The Grand Deception

Passing by the grand facade of the National Assembly on Tuesday evening, the mass of students had a fine opportunity to cast a few derisive slogans but, instead, did not even acknowledge its presence. It was a sign of the times, this complete indifference, omitting from consideration an institution that for ten years had bathed in its own incapacity. The legislators inside, however, did not reciprocate this indifference. In a moment of consensus, rare since the advent of the Fifth Republic, the majority and the opposition minority agreed that, on the morrow, the Assembly should hold an emergency session on the student issue and call in Peyrefitte to tell his story.

Peyrefitte recited a lengthy history of the movement. Then, perhaps moved by the Assembly's sense of urgency, perhaps impressed by the march of the day before, or simply tired of the constant appeals from professors to yield to the student demands, Peyrefitte backed down: "University courses will resume when professors and students are capable of maintaining order despite the agitators, and that may be tomorrow afternoon."[12]

Rain drizzled in Paris on a third day of continued student demonstrations. They were dug in at the Faculty of Sciences, east of the Boulevard St. Michel on the left bank. There, they heard of Peyrefitte's announcement that the Sorbonne would reopen on the morrow on the condition that the students behave properly—a condition vague

---

12. "Les déliberations du Conseil des Ministres," *Le Monde,* 9 Mai 1968, p. 8.

enough to give him the option of reasserting his authority if he deemed it necessary. Few took him very seriously, and those who did considered his proposal insufficient. It was unthinkable, at this point, to accept a settlement for less than the three major demands. The twenty thousand students gathered under the column supports of the Faculty of Sciences demonstrated once more in a now familiar pattern: a tour around the Latin Quarter, dispersion at 11:00 P.M. and an occasional skirmish until morning.

Late on Thursday morning Rector Roche finally agreed that the Sorbonne might be opened that afternoon, reaffirming the conditional proposal of the day before. UNEF contented itself with dispersing the demonstrators during the day and ordering all to appear before the Sorbonne for the opening of the doors. As the day waned, an attendant mass gathered along the Boulevard St. Michel, sitting down on the pavement. Shortly, a meeting was under way.

Four o'clock passed, then five, and six. Students started drifting down the boulevard, distraught and incensed, while the Sorbonne remained closed within an increasingly wide and armored hedge of CRS. What had happened in the time between Peyrefitte's address to the National Assembly on Wednesday and his mysterious refusal to follow through on his proposal on Thursday? There existed a certain discord between two very crucial ministers: Peyrefitte of National Education and Fouchet of the Interior and National Security. Fouchet had been convinced by police officials that it was best to open the doors of the Sorbonne and let the students make trouble within the walls of the university rather than in the street. The logic of this policy was simple: inside the campus, student protest would drown in its own chaotic democracy. Peyrefitte, on the other hand, was clearly displeased. He could have expected as much from Fouchet, with whom he had long been at odds. Peyrefitte's domain was the Sorbonne, and he no more wanted the students stirring up dust in his house than Fouchet wanted dust in his streets. As the movement continued to increase in magnitude, and as repeated visits of distinguished professors continued to press him, Peyrefitte dreaded more and more "giving in." A defeat at the hands of the students was bad enough, but defeat within the cabinet was shameful. It was not until Wednesday afternoon, faced with a displeased Assembly, that he had offered his conditional proposal.

There was still a further problem. Peyrefitte had unfortunately not consulted with De Gaulle before announcing on Wednesday his intention to open the Sorbonne, and when de Gaulle found out that Peyrefitte had relaxed his position without his approval, he did not hide his displeasure. How could Peyrefitte undertake such an adventure without clearing it with him? So, regretting his announcement since Wednesday night, Peyrefitte hoped to regain favor with de Gaulle by retracting his conditional promise to open the Sorbonne.

He found this pretext on Thursday afternoon, thanks to the several thousand students who had impatiently crowded around the Sorbonne. Cohn-Bendit, Geismar, and Sauvageot were soon using the portable microphone at this spontaneous meeting. Roche telephoned Peyrefitte and said that the students were talking of occupying the Sorbonne. Peyrefitte then had all the information he needed, and shortly after 6:00 P.M. he agreed to open Nanterre but reversed his decision regarding the Sorbonne.[13] No grand opening, just a grand deception.

Friday Red II

By the end of the week, de Gaulle and Peyrefitte began to pay the price for an inconsistent and self-contradictory approach to the student movement. On the one hand, they had refused to admit the gravity of the situation, while on the other they continued to increase the police presence; their aim was, in effect, to publicly belittle the movement's magnitude while, under the guise of keeping order, demoralize the students with a severe repression. This simply added up to ignoring the students in one instant and striking them in the next. The students were not the least bit demoralized by the repression. If anything, they were incited and the public remained unconvinced by the government's insistence that the protests amounted to a "handful of agitators" and "professional hoodlums."

The government's policy had undeniably failed. With the Sorbonne still closed and students still imprisoned, there was not a hint of de-escalation. In the conspicuous absence of Prime Minister Pompidou (in Afghanistan since Tuesday) Minister Joxe, serving in his absence, made a further token attempt to appease the students. He offered two of the three demands: immediate withdrawal of police from the Sorbonne and its reopening. Unsurprisingly, his offer was refused.

Once again, UNEF called a demonstration, the fourth of the week. It began outside the Latin Quarter and headed for the Seine but, since all bridges were blocked, no other route was possible except, oddly

---

13. The circumstances and the motivations for Peyrefitte's decision are obscure. See "La Revolution de Mai," *L'Express,* Supplément Exceptionnel, Mai 1968.

enough, the one leading toward the Sorbonne. Thirty to forty thousand students Friday evening found themselves marching up the Boulevard St. Michel. There, as excitement mounted, signposts were lifted from the streets, and the demonstration continued to increase in size. What to do? UNEF had forbidden contact with the police, and enforced this with a large student security force of its own, but where to go? It seemed that the students had come to the end of the road at the corner of Rue Gay-Lussac and Boulevard St. Michel, and there they did what came natural—they sat down. Cohn-Bendit explained it later at length:

> On Wednesday, when the demonstration arrived on the upper part of the Boulevard St. Michel, someone asked the students to disperse. We were against this, but that was not important. What was important was the way in which the students received this command: they were floored. I saw some who cried and said: 'OK, so where do we go now? Do we give up? Have we come here for nothing? We have had a thousand wounded in two days already and we're supposed to march from the Bastille to the Place de la Republique and then return home?[14] What good is that?' And that was the sentiment of almost all of the young people there, not only the students but also the young workers who had come to join us.
>
> So on Wednesday night, the March 22 Movement together with the other organizations, agreed: we can no longer remain as we are, the movement has its own dynamism and the young people have decided to fight . . . it is necessary to give them something.
>
> Friday, at Denfert Rochereau, at the moment when the demonstration was formed, we organizers discussed at length what we were going to do and where to go. It was no longer a matter of a simple procession—the students would not have understood—but neither were we looking deliberately for trouble with the police because we could not send students to get massacred. Our idea was then to occupy a specific place, peacefully, and stay there until our three demands had been satisfied: liberation of our comrades, withdrawal of the police from the Latin Quarter and the reopening of the Sorbonne.

---

14. This was the standard itinerary of Paris demonstrations, considered impotent by the speaker.

We had planned to occupy the Palais de Justice, but the difficulties were too great. Some had thought also of occupying the Place Vendôme but, there too, there were many problems. Finally we went toward the Latin Quarter, and the police let us pass. If there had been blockades, we would have gone on to occupy another place. In fact, the police directed us toward the Latin Quarter. Having arrived at the Boulevard St. Michel, we stopped and the students sat on the ground, while we discussed what we could do. Then, when we went farther up the Boulevard, toward the Place de Luxembourg, I saw that the students had begun already to take up the cobblestones and to make barricades. When everyone began to do so, it became evident that this, in fact, was the best tactic.[15]

The basic idea of the tactic was to abandon the mass demonstration and split up into small groups so that each street to the south of the Sorbonne would be occupied by some students. Shortly after 9:00, the students dispersed throughout the area east of Boulevard St. Michel and began to rip up signs and fences to construct barricades. Once the spirit of defiance was in the air, the barricades cropped up like weeds, a total of ten observed within the first hour in the environs of the Sorbonne and Panthéon alone. Bit by bit, the process of occupation with fortifications spread into all the small streets.

It became evident that this night would only resolve itself in a surrender of the administrators to the students' demands or a massacre of the students. Roche realized this and sent a message to the crowd that he was ready to "receive representatives of the students of the Sorbonne" in order to examine with them the conditions under which courses could resume.

Roche finally and properly panicked; he realized that somebody had to stop the violence that threatened. But he was the only one. The ministers were still very much in their own stew, and were hardly prepared to deal directly with student demands. Peyrefitte was astounded by what he had started and would have liked to wash his hands of it all without, of course, angering the General. Fouchet, hour by hour, as impatient after his own fashion as the students, wanted to

---

15. D. Cohn-Bendit, op. cit., p. 32.

abandon the talks and disperse the students. From barricade to barricade, the minister's informants reported a "climate of violence."

At midnight, finally, Roche received the representatives, among whom were Cohn-Bendit, three professors, and two members of UNEF. Peyrefitte, with the Minister of Justice, meanwhile followed the events by transistor radio, and heard that Roche had received Cohn-Bendit in his office. His blood went cold; Roche had admitted an *extremist* into the negotiations!

Peyrefitte called Roche's office on the phone.

P.   Rector, this is Peyrefitte, tell me, exactly, who is in your office?

R.   A delegation from UNEF.

P.   And Cohn-Bendit, he is there too, isn't he?

R.   I do not believe so, Monsieur le Ministre.

P.   Do you not have before you a student with red hair and a round face?

R.   Well, yes indeed.

P.   That, sir, is Cohn-Bendit. Monsieur le Recteur, I want to speak with you in private; please go into the next room.[16]

Thus, with a decisive and burlesque conversation, the last possibility to reconcile with the students and avoid violence ended. Peyrefitte, no doubt chagrined at the idea of negotiating with Cohn-Bendit, told Roche there would be no changes at that time. The delegation invited Roche to accompany them to the streets, to see for himself the storm that was brewing. He refused, preferring to stay by the phone waiting for a new contact with the Minister. The delegation returned to the streets alone, where there were now sixty barricades, red flags flying, and crowds celebrating their fortresses with joyous fever.

Meanwhile, behind the barricades, a curious thing happened. The residents of these streets, enclosed in fortresses of cobblestones, began to help the students in various ways with great enthusiasm. Older gentlemen offered advice on the construction area nearby, where an army of demonstrators supplied themselves with crude weapons. Food and drink, blankets, even mattresses were tossed out of windows.

---

16. J. Alia, Y. le Vaillant, and L. Rioux, "Les Sentiers de la déroute," *Le Nouvel Observateur*, no. 183, 15–21 Mai 1968, p. 27.

Many residents watched their cars being turned over and set sideways for barricades without objection.[17]

The occupation went well until 2:00 A.M., when fighting began, but then the police spared no one. An unexpected tenacity in the demonstrators struck pangs of fear into the squads, who every few minutes saw one of their members taken out by a well-aimed cobblestone. What was originally their duty was now fueled by anger. At some point, they began to use a different sort of grenade, containing far more noxious chemicals than ordinary tear gas. Police wrenched victims off stretchers, simultaneously beating the wounded as well as the Red Cross. Radio stations pitched in and pleaded help for a blinded girl behind a barricade, closed off by the police who refused to let her be taken out.[18] A savage frenzy consumed the police force, whose leaders admitted a loss of command over their men.

Shortly, the air was saturated with tear gas mixed with waves of smoke rising from the hundreds of overturned cars burning out of control; it was impossible to breathe. The demonstrators retreated from one barricade to another with each attack of the police. From frustration to frenzy, the police took to attacking sympathetic neighbors, launching tear gas grenades into open windows along the streets, and chasing students into the apartments where they sought refuge. The demonstrators in turn headed for the roofs of buildings, preparing to toss Molotov cocktails onto the approaching police.

Inopportune as it was, the government intervened toward 4:00 A.M., well after any chance of remedying the situation had passed, and made it known that dialogue was always possible. Few people could help but be struck by the absurdity of this communication. A particularly harsh response came from two Nobel prize recipients and a host of other professors, who threatened their resignation from the French university if the police did not withdraw. The radio stations pleaded for a cessation of hostilities and residents likewise attempted to intervene between the police and the students.

Their efforts were to little avail. A professor who was located in a Red Cross post, improvised in a garden near the Sorbonne, attempted to prevent the intervention of the police in the building where the

---

17. See "Nuit dramatique au Quartier Latin," *Le Monde,* 12–13 Mai 1968, p. 1, for an excellent description of this night's events.

18. News Broadcast, Radio Luxembourg, May 12, 1973.

wounded received treatment. The police responded with several blows, and entered the infirmary to drag out the wounded. Many others, in the process of evacuating the wounded, also found themselves more severely victimized than their patients. One medical aide who had volunteered his services in a temporary infirmary on the street Gay-Lussac, rendered the following remarkable account of a night he would not soon forget:

> At the time of the major attack which hit us about 2:15 A.M., we had set up an infirmary in an apartment off Gay-Lussac where we received wounded students. At some point it became necessary to evacuate our entire operation to another location down the street. With some help, I stayed to care for the wounded who continued to arrive. Then there was a savage attack, with the worst sort of gas, leaving us no choice but to quit our temporary post. We wanted to make it out by way of the roof, but police spotted us and shot gas bombs up at us. I made my way down successfully, and when I did, I found three wounded policemen lying on the ground. My duty obliged me to help them, which I did. A student was lying not far away, and when I subsequently went to him, I was violently beaten, kicked to the ground, and taken to a paddy wagon and to the station where once again I was kicked and beaten. I stayed there until the next afternoon when one of the policemen whom I had healed let me go. When I was released and as I left the station, seeing some used tear gas bombs, I picked some up; but immediately I was again seized by the police, beaten again, and put into a cell. This time I saw some shocking things. At the station the wounded were not only left without care but were refused care, and when I tried to help, I was violently prevented. In my cell, I saw a student who had been there two days without food or water. Ten hours later, I was released.[19]

Groups of students resisted until 5:00 in the morning when Cohn-Bendit appealed on the radio to disperse. At 6:00, on the hour, a new shift of CRS replaced the night shift, one of the few regularities that this day would see. A car used by a private radio station, which had continued on the air past its normal hour to serve the demonstration by

---

19. "L'Assaut des forces de police," *Le Monde,* 12–13 Mai 1968, p. 3.

reporting the action, was parked and its two reporters were asleep. For the rest of the morning, the streets were left to the police who continued to chase the remaining demonstrators into corners, to street repairmen who replaced the cobblestones, and to a curious early morning audience, bums and reporters who were soon to tell their respective worlds of the previous night's events.

Saturday's newspapers unfolded before the eyes of shocked readers:

LATIN QUARTER TRANSFORMED INTO BATTLEFIELD.
POLICE LAUNCH ASSAULT ON 60 BARRICADES.
HUNDREDS WOUNDED AND ARRESTED, CARS BURNED, APARTMENTS OCCUPIED.
PARISIAN POPULATION SUPPORTS DEMONSTRATORS IN GENERAL STRIKE MONDAY.

This night of unexpected repression brought the students a massive wave of support. Weeklong marches, along with vociferous condemnations of bourgeois universities and consumer society had served to kindle grievances lying smoldering in many sectors of society, spreading a chain of powder throughout the nation. It might have been diffused and forgotten if met with conciliation, but it was met with a repression so brutal the fuse was lit.[20]

French grievances were many, and the willingness of the French to protest proverbial. For the first time in a long while, following the second Friday night encounter, all the disparate forces of the French left appealed in union for a massive demonstration in the Latin Quarter. Even the Communist Party and General Confederation of Workers (CGT) tendered a distinctly favorable response, calling for a general strike to accompany the march on Monday.[21]

Fitful, and sensing a rapid deterioration of its control, the government made a first, positive attempt at conciliation. Georges Pompidou

---

20. "Les grenades utilisées pour les operations contre les rassemblements," *Le Monde*, 12–13 Mai 1968, p. 2. See also, "Les techniques des manifestations," *Le Nouvel Observateur*, 15–21 Mai 1968, p. 29.

21. The French union system is complicated. The majority of workers are nonunionized but small unions exist in most large businesses and government agencies and are often able to lead strikes in which the nonunionized workers participate. The three main unions are, in order of size, the Communist-led CGT, the French Democratic Confederation of Labor (CFDT), and Worker Force (FO). There are also unions of farmers, executives, and other categories not usually unionized in the United States.

had returned from a weeklong visit to Afghanistan. None of France's ministers, excepting Peyrefitte in some rare moments, had up to this point even acknowledged a climate of serious unrest. In returning to find some five hundred wounded in a battle that recalled in miniature the Commune of 1871, Georges Pompidou at least realized that the situation was an emergency.[22]

What could he do that the others had not been able to do up to now, and particularly at this moment, squeezed between Friday night and Monday morning? He simply capitulated, granting the students' every demand: amnesty for all arrested students, liberation of the Sorbonne, withdrawal of police, and even a promise that students inconvenienced by the weeks' disorder would be offered special arrangements for taking the exam.[23] Pompidou had hoped, by capitulating, to produce a miracle, to turn ashes into honey, to return the students to their homes and schools, content and appeased by their victory. But for all its good appearances his action was at best a sleight of hand, clever only because no one had dared to try it before; however, the real solution to the problem was to change the magician and not the tricks.

At this late date, Pompidou's capitulation went largely unheeded. His intervention did little to douse an already flaming blaze. The die of a popular movement had already been cast by the working world, which decided to respond to the student appeal, by the university, which learned that a revolution is fought for and not voted on, and by the police whose actions undermined Pompidou's credibility.

Monday May 13

It was spring in Paris, and de Gaulle's international maneuvering against American imperialism had culminated in one of the greatest coups of his diplomatic career—bringing the Vietnam peace negotiations to his lovely capital city. On Monday, May 13, talks between Americans and Vietnamese were to open, but de Gaulle had little time to strut about; the fierce encounter of the state and the students on Friday night had awakened his population to an "internal imperialism" for which they blamed him. A general strike on Monday the 13th paralyzed the

---

22. On March 18, 1871, in the wake of French defeat in the Franco-Prussian War, revolutionaries seized power in Paris and ruled the city for seventy-two days. The famous "Commune of Paris" became the symbol of working-class revolution.

23. "Je demande à tous de coopérer à l'apaisment," *Le Monde*, 15 Mai 1968, p. 3.

country, while a demonstration of over a million marched through the streets in sympathy with the students.

As fate would have it, May 13 also commemorated the tenth anniversary of the coup that brought de Gaulle to power, a fact the demonstrators were only too delighted to remember as they marched: TEN YEARS, THAT'S ENOUGH. DE GAULLE TO THE ARCHIVES. DE GAULLE TO THE REST HOME. The march brought to the surface an immense undercurrent of demands long ignored, for greater political and economic rights for workers, democratic reform of the university, full employment, transformation of the economic system by and for the people. These demands gave a deeper purpose to the revolutionary action that, in the coming weeks, seriously shook de Gaulle's regime.

While this day proved that students and workers could present a common front, a fault also appeared in the foundation of their movement. The alliance of Communist Party and union leaders with the students was a contentious and difficult one. A movement built on this alliance inevitably had two contrary faces. The one embodied the energy of student leaders, diffused and avowedly immoderate; this student energy had driven the police to commit brutalities that inspired a popular demonstration unequaled in the history of the Fifth Republic. The other aspect, that of the Communist Party and France's major union, the General Confederation of Workers (CGT), presented a reformist, almost moderate face.[24]

Police repression against the students had united the left-wing forces, something heretofore impossible; the Communists and the students muted their mutual hostility in the hope of overthrowing de Gaulle and the capitalist system. Had this proved feasible, the two faces of the movement might have been an asset, uniting the massive following of the one and the youthful spirit of the other to produce a general revolution.

As it was, the two faces of the movement proved incompatible right from the start; even during the march on Monday, they regarded each other with distrust. Disagreement had first arisen on Saturday, following a lengthy debate on the direction of the march. Once this was settled, union leaders showed themselves reluctant to let student leaders stand in front, while students insisted they not be outplaced;

---

24. Julien Fanjeaux, "Les Grèvistes," *L'Evénement*, Juillet–Aout, 1968, pp. 48–54.

after all, students argued, union leaders did not fight for first place on the barricades.

As the march reached its destination, Cohn-Bendit bobbed in and out of the crowds with his megaphone, pleading for a continuation of the march, while at the same time the loudspeaker of the CGT called for dispersion, drowning out his voice. There was great confusion. Only a meager 5000 students followed the leader of the March 22 Movement toward the Eiffel Tower for a meeting.[25] This incident, although inconspicuous and of short duration, must be considered one of the critical moments of the movement. It symbolized not only the feud between Cohn-Bendit and the Communist Party, but also the utter incompatibility of the student movement and the established left parties, which eventually would destroy the movement.

It would be a mistake to presume though that on Monday reform prevailed over revolution simply because union and party leaders prevailed over Cohn-Bendit for an afternoon. After such a demonstration of unity and force as the march on Monday, neither past history nor present conflict among the forces of the left could diminish the hope of change, and a network of revolutionary activity began taking root even as the demonstration dispersed into the streets.

The student front returned to claim their Sorbonne, occupied it and turned it into a fortress of revolutionary culture; two days later they seized the Théâtre de l'Odéon to purge it of its elite culture and declare it open to the people, in the service of the revolution. Workers in the following days occupied their factories without waiting for union orders, progressively paralyzing all industrial activity.

Television and radio personnel, long subjected to political censorship, organized their own strikes, allowing only a minimum of programs on the air and depriving the government of its most effective instrument of persuasion. A flurry of activity among leftist politicians initiated legislative measures: the release of all arrested demonstrators, a motion of censure against de Gaulle, and a pile of parliamentary invectives.

What happened in the next few weeks made some of the better days of many lives. The streets of Paris slowly emptied of gas-starved cars, and pedestrians filled the empty space they left behind. Formerly busy bureaucrats, housewives, shopkeepers, and grocery men inter-

---

25. Gérard Desseigne, "Syndicats et Etudiants," *Le Monde,* 17 Mai 1968, p. 6.

rupted the banal process of making a living to find out what life was all about. As each of the institutions came under revolutionary control (first the Sorbonne, then the Théâtre de l'Odéon, the factories, all the schools of Paris, and soon all of France), everyone on the streets of the Latin Quarter rejoiced and spoke feverishly of what would happen next.

If the pace of this history slows down at this point, it is only by pen of the author and not of the events, for there was never a dull hour. It so happened that, in the first week, anybody could be everywhere at any one time, since everything of major interest took place within a few minutes' walking distance. In the following weeks, however, this was not true. The pace did not slow down, but centers of action multiplied, so that to follow the movement in all its aspects one had to revolutionize his time as well as his politics. The reader must do the same.

The normal day of a revolutionary would begin at a nearby factory, hanging on the outside gates reinforcing the workers' determination (which meant lauding the barricades and condemning the CGT). Then to the Sorbonne for the afternoon, picking up on impromptu conferences in the courtyard, attending scheduled debates in lecture halls, reflecting on police brutality at displays of photos of the fighting, taking notes, and seeking out some new corner of the movement in a committee, perhaps concerning Che Guevera and Freud on human liberation. All Paris schools needed help: Les Beaux Arts (National School of the Arts) appealed for personnel to paste up posters turned out in their studios; the school of medicine called for volunteer first-aid crews; the Sorbonne needed sweepers; all needed members for occupation committees. Nights were spent at the "Ex-Odéon Théâtre Populaire" where revolutionary jargon, poetry, and skirmishes with police crowded the stage until morning.

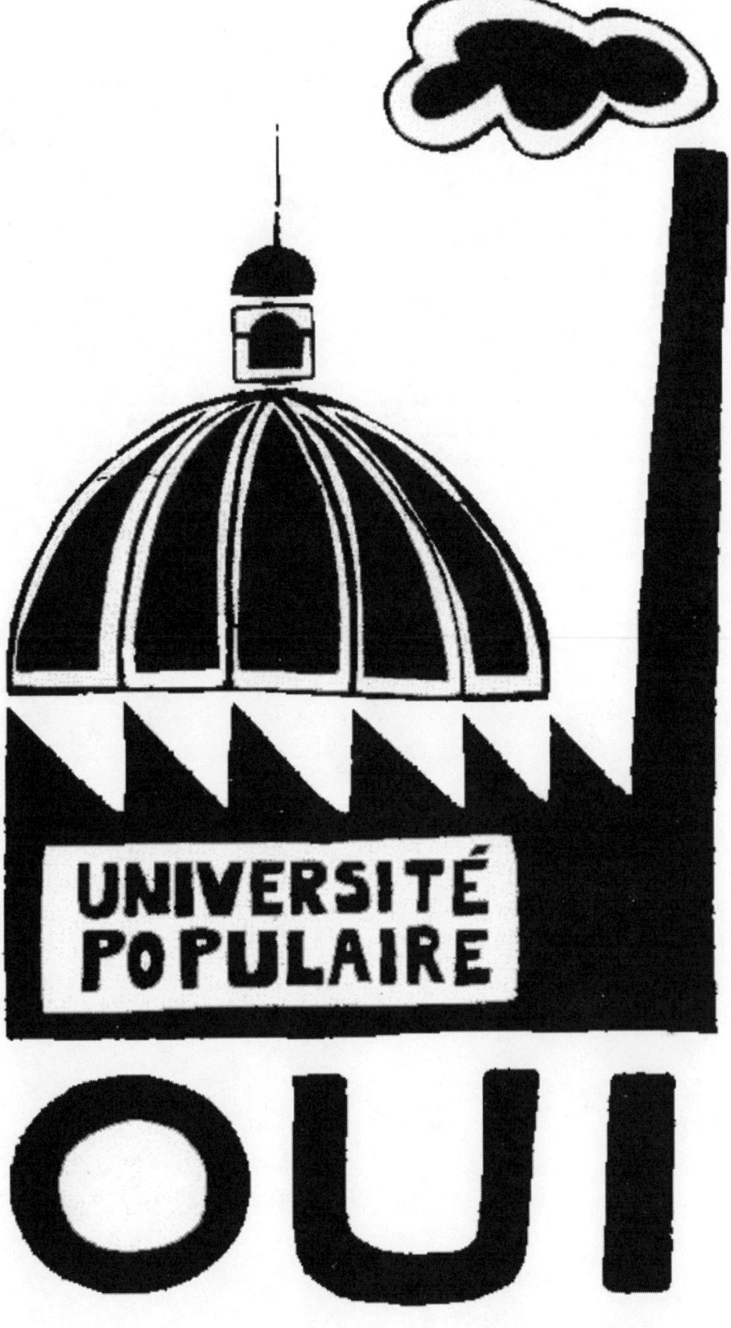
UNIVERSITÉ
POPULAIRE
OUI

PART II. SOCIETY VERSUS THE STATE

From the Sorbonne to Renault—Students and Workers

Leaders of the General Confederation of Workers (CGT) no doubt imagined that by marching with the students on Monday, they had shown at least a token sympathy with the victims of repression and fulfilled their "insurrectionary" obligation; they hardly took seriously the idea of a student-worker alliance, neither for reform nor for revolution, still less Cohn-Bendit's appeal to the workers to occupy their factories and make a revolution their leaders considered untimely.

But out of the unpredictable evolution of the May movement came, if not an actual alliance, at least a parallel determination to challenge the entire society, shared by students and workers, young ones in particular. The issue was no longer simply reforms or salary hikes, but total opposition to state authority.[26] The consequences of this parallel brought a shocking surprise to officials of the CGT in the four days of May 14–18, when, in response to the students' struggle, over one hundred thousand workers in thirteen major factories went on strike and occupied their plants without a word from the unions. The first was Sud-Aviation on Tuesday night, twenty-four hours after the Monday demonstration.[27] There young workers seized control of the workshops and imprisoned the director, reportedly with assistance from students. On Wednesday the grounds of a large naval construction firm ceased operation, and on Thursday the entire Renault complex hoisted a red flag above its gates.

The process was generally the same: initiative taken by young radical elements, occasional but only minor objections from older workers, a notable presence of students discussing and dispensing information to the workers, and conspicuous lack of union leadership. By

---

26. Jacques Julliard, "Syndicalisme révolutionnaire et révolution étudiante," *Esprit,* Juin–Juillet 1968, pp. 1037–1045.

27. For more on the strike at Sud-Aviation, see "Nantes: A Whole Town Discovers the Power of the People" in the Documents section.

Friday afternoon the courtship between workers and students was unmistakable. A new phase of the May revolution had begun. The Communist Party and the CGT were understandably ill at ease; a revolution was brewing that defied any traditional Marxian interpretation. Workers were the followers and not the initiators of this strike, inspired not by an oppressed class, but by students, many of whom had never known the burdens but only the advantages of capitalism. It was to the Sorbonne, to an alternative to union leadership, to advocates of the anarchistic theory of self-management, that the workers turned. After the CGT released a statement on Wednesday saying "make your desires fit your realities,"[28] a slogan was inscribed on the walls of the Sorbonne, reversing the rusty wisdom of the past: TAKE YOUR DESIRES FOR YOUR REALITIES.

Renault Boulogne-Billancourt, Renault's major factory, a bastion of the CGT, with gray walls, and heavy grilled doors, had long been in the vanguard of the workers' movement. There everyone spoke about the barricades in the factories, the young especially. And when they saw the students demonstrate for them, they recognized that there was something fishy with the unions. Thursday afternoon, in one of the workshops at Renault, a fellow said, "I've had it," and he quit. "You crazy?" asked his buddy. Then his buddy quit, and the whole workshop quit, from chain to chain, from post to post, everywhere. In half an hour, the entire factory had quit and decided to occupy their grounds like the students. The unions had to follow the movement, but they ordered that students should not be allowed into the factory.

By Saturday, two days after its occupation, despite its grim external appearance, there was a sense of victory inside. It is rare, the workers say, to talk among their fellows; they seldom have time in the dreary laboring day. When, at 2:00 Saturday morning, small groups of workers came to join the occupation, everyone talked, and high spirits reigned. One young man in his mid-twenties mounted a pile of boxes behind the factory's sliding doors and gained the attention of a nearby crowd: "It is slavery here, we're worse off than animals." He formed one of the initial groups of workers who had "had enough," who had said, despite all the warnings, "Let's quit." And today, they had won, or at least almost won; the red flag floated on top of the building and all of France had gone on strike.

The young man continued:

---

28. "Un appel de la CGT," *Le Monde*, 17 Mai 1968, p. 6.

Listen, after work, I'm beat. I come home, it takes me two hours, I arrive, eat and sleep. It's nice to have cultural attractions, real nice, but we are too tired to even go. All the young workers like myself have had enough. What do we want? A piece of the cake. It's normal. We work, so we want part of the cake. The old unionized workers say we are foolish, that we did not see '36. They say, wait. Wait for the unions to give the word and things will be all right. Well, the unions want to control everything and do nothing. Up to Monday, the unions told us in leaflets that the students were stupid, and then the next day, bravo, everybody is for the students! All of a sudden we realized what the unions were all about. We saw how the students fought and what they got. It worked. Cars burned, material damaged, all that is unimportant. What is important is that you can't have an omelette without breaking some eggs. We'd all be where we always were if it weren't for the barricades.

As for me, I like the students; I believe they should be allowed to enter and talk to us, but the unions are afraid. I have never done any college; I can't speak very well. I'm afraid to go to the Sorbonne. Yet the students I meet seem OK. Not at all provocateurs like the unions say.[29]

In the early days of the week, Tuesday and Wednesday, a few workers began to frequent the Sorbonne. Direct democracy had been declared there, which meant in principle that no one should be denied the right to speak, while in practice most speakers were equally ignored. But the worker, more than anyone, was a valued visitor. To him, for the first time, fell the privilege of the platform at the Sorbonne. And in return, as the workers occupied their factories, the students brought the Sorbonne to them. On Thursday afternoon, UNEF and SNEsup announced a demonstration from the Sorbonne to the Renault factory at Boulogne-Billancourt, seized early that morning by young workers such as the one quoted above. The meeting was necessarily bizarre as the factory was closed to outsiders, the CGT having distributed leaflets discouraging contact with "irresponsible students." Police appeared from time to time. Regardless of the obstacles, it was a great event, symbolizing a second wind for the movement. The students carried a

---

29. "Le socialisme mais avec qui?" *Le Nouvel Observateur*, 30 Mai 1968, Edition Speciale, p. 8.

big banner with the plea: TAKE FROM OUR FRAGILE HANDS THE STRUGGLE AGAINST THE REGIME. Contact was made and the courtship nourished; workers gathered on street corners, met students on changing shifts, and slowly the protective coating of the Party and CGT melted away.

The next day, another march led five thousand students to Renault, after which factories began to send appeals to the Sorbonne for manpower to reinforce their picket lines. By Monday, strikes had reached into every sector of the economy. A total of ten million workers had indeed taken the movement from the fragile hands of the students. Faced with a 'fait accompli,' the CGT could do little else but help spread the strikes and pretend to court the students, particularly given the emergence of a new division in union politics. France's second largest union, the French Democratic Confederation of Labor (CFDT), had expressed full support for the student movement and had come out for workers' power in the factories, paralleling the demand for "student power" in the Sorbonne.

In extending their movement to the working population, students had accomplished what the major unions had considered practically impossible, what the Communist Party had declared theoretically absurd, and what the government had never imagined. A week had now passed since the memorable march of Monday May 13. Factories all buzzed with discussion under the newly raised red flag and, since that Monday night a week ago, the concept of cobblestones, those instruments and symbols of revolution, remained under constant debate at the Sorbonne. Pompidou, who continued to accuse a few agitators of irresponsibility, and de Gaulle, who had passed Tuesday to Saturday of this decisive week on a state visit to Roumania, seemed not to notice that France tottered more and more on the brink of national crisis.

A La Sorbonne

The Boulevard St. Michel, Monday evening, May 13, had been a scene of exaltation as students filed into the gates and reclaimed the Sorbonne. In the hot night, thousands of people penetrated into the courtyard, where groups gathered under the severe regard of Victor Hugo and Louis Pasteur, two comrades in stone, now sporting red and black flags, respectively. Here, where French culture passed from adult to youth, where students were filtered from exam to job, a generation installed itself with the aim of reversing the normal process of "l'entrée dans la vie," and attacked the society they were supposed to enter.

Every amphitheater had been packed on this first night of the occupation. In one hall, the debate lagged briefly and an older professor, drawn and concerned, resolved to introduce a note of dissension: to put politics in the university, he said, was to introduce agitation and disorder, and both were incompatible with serious studies. He could not make himself heard. His words might have rung true before the Events but now he stepped down unsuccessfully, yielding to the majority that ruled by the energy of revolt, and let the debate return to its already habitual bedlam.

In another lecture hall, the stage was full and the audience noisy when a familiar voice boomed into the microphone. "Go ahead say it, what you just said, say it again in front of everyone." It was Cohn-Bendit again, on the first night of the Free Sorbonne. A young man came forward: "I speak as a militant communist; don't forget that 100 years ago, it was the Communist Party which fought for the liberation of the working class. It was the party which led the Spanish Civil War. And it was the party which fought in the Resistance and suffered the deaths."

Cohn-Bendit took the microphone again and began apologetically:

> A minute ago, I was a little excited. I was wrong. This comrade who has just spoken is an excellent comrade. He worked against me at Nanterre, called me all kinds of names, but I don't care. It is our political direction which counts, or more importantly, our lack of it for the moment. It is necessary to question all political leadership, particularly that of the Communist Party, in view of the efficacy of spontaneous action in the streets and the continuation of the movement.[30]

What was unique about the Sorbonne, to which Cohn-Bendit had referred, what made it the model of the entire revolt, was its refusal of all leadership. People normally fear revolutions, on any scale, not necessarily because they fear disorder (for, in fact, disorder is often exhilarating), but because they fear the severity of a new order that succeeds the abandon. On the reverse side of the wild card that is revolution lurks the constant threat of dictatorship. In the French movement, which was directed specifically against an authoritarian regime, the

---

30. "Naissances d'une université critique au Quartier Latin," *Le Monde,* 15 Mai 1968, p. 8.

participants were not about to allow another system to install itself where the previous one had cruelly ruled.

Herein was the beauty of the Sorbonne of these times: it fought not only against the regime, but against the revolution, or at least the revolutionary tradition. It was the libertarian valve of the movement, open wide, imposing no order and very little opinion, refusing no one the floor, denying nothing but constraint. Programs on permanent protest, on the critical university, on the maintenance of the Sorbonne as an arena of direct democracy, were conceived as barriers against the eventuality of any and all discipline. Here was the revolution within the revolution, a radically new model proposed to the twentieth century, a revolution without dictatorship, ruled only by imagination.[31]

All the while, jazz blared from the steps of the chapel in the outer courtyard; Dave Brubeck and Mao Tse-Tung were there together in a spectacle of liberation. Many residents of the Latin Quarter, who a few nights back had thrown water onto the barricades to wash away the gas and given the young revolutionaries refuge in their homes, came for the first time to the Sorbonne. A reception desk received visitors who wanted to know where they could go, how they could help out. Many who came for an evening stayed a week. On the third floor was a dormitory for permanent residents. Elsewhere, a nursery for young children was opened, and a food service with volunteer sweepers to deal with the dialectic of dirt.

The walls of the Sorbonne, for so long deaf and dumb to the problems of the emerging consumer society, now rebounded with Marx and Lenin, Freud and Che Guevara, offering some lessons of their own: IT IS FORBIDDEN TO FORBID. ALL POWER TO THE IMAGINATION. ANSWER EXAMS WITH QUESTIONS. WE WANT A WORLD, NEW AND ORIGINAL. WE REFUSE A WORLD WHERE THE ASSURANCE OF NOT DYING FROM HUNGER IS EXCHANGED FOR THE RISK OF DYING FROM BOREDOM.

Boredom and repetition were cardinal sins. In one lecture hall a standing committee led a discussion on "permanent protest"; in another, someone read a dissertation on the role of the orgy in the Roman Empire and Puritanism in China. The question was to define what cultures and what societies most fully permitted the total liberation of the human being, and in the process no institution went unchallenged.

---

31. For an idea of the Sorbonne's new thinking, see "The Amnesty of Blinded Eyes" in the Documents section.

Why should knowledge privilege a teacher over a student or parentage give a father the right to discipline his son? How to replace boss with worker and government with the people?

Out of the sentiment if not always out of the sense of the impassioned discussion, two tendencies become clear: for some, the now liberated university should combat society; for others, a new university should be created within the existing society. The former envisioned a university that would serve as a political base, widening the possibilities for spontaneous mobilization of a movement that would carry the revolution toward a new kind of socialism. The latter envisioned a more fruitful union of the university and society, a return to order and reforms through negotiation and legislation.

These two tendencies corresponded to the two faces of the larger movement: the Communist Party versus the *enragés*, the CGT versus the student-worker alliance. And, as always, tension between these two faces, reformist and revolutionary, weighed heavily on the proceedings. Like a tug of war, the one in its maximalism fought against the other's compromises.

It was in such an atmosphere that the issue of exams was constantly debated. Here was the strongest point of reformist resistance to extremist pressure. The reformists appealed to the 511,000 students in France who stood to lose an entire year's credit if exams were discarded in the wake of the movement. The revolutionaries, for their part, could not have cared less. From the very beginning, the March 22 Movement had advocated a general boycott. Their analysis was simple: the exam is the key to the entire system, the goal of all scholarly work. To crack the exams, they reasoned, was to crack that system. They also recognized that if exams were scheduled, the movement would dissipate as everyone returned home with their books and manuals.

Discussions were long and heated before an accord was reached. Finally it was decided that the question of exams should be submitted to a commission of students and professors who would construct a completely new system to be administered in the fall. It was a victory for the revolutionaries, and one of them appropriately proclaimed it in a clear space on a Sorbonne wall: WE WILL HAVE GOOD MASTERS WHEN EACH WILL BE HIS OWN.

The schism continued. Reformists' meetings were calm, at appointed hours, mostly in the upper stories, sometimes bordering on the concrete and practical. It was here that the creative anarchy of the street disciplined itself to the task of reforming the university. Meanwhile, revolutionaries held meetings around the clock, debating the union of workers and students, the degradation of the Communist Party, and ways of maintaining the popular energy generated by a week of street action.

This last concern was obsessive. The movement, by its very success, had played into the hands of the government and removed itself from the public eye. In fighting with the police, the students and their allies had tapped an undauntable source of energy; but, in the Sorbonne, the only force they had to contend with was their own incapacity, the only victims of their combativeness were themselves. How now to prevent a paradoxical hardening of the revolutionary arteries?

Au Théâtre de l'Odéon

The first resolution of this paradox resulted in one of the most spectacular achievements of the month. Sometime after 11:00 on Wednesday night, May 15, one thousand students entered the sacred halls of Théâtre de l'Odéon, symbolic monument to French culture. Clambering over red felt chairs, onto the stage, they conquered the famed Theater of France and declared it the "Ex-ODÉON, in the service of the people." The coffers of revolutionary emotion, starved for three days, were once again filled and another night was spent in celebration and victory.

Opening night of the revolutionary theater featured Cohn-Bendit and Jean-Louis Barrault, France's most famous actor and theater director, before an overflow crowd that reached twice the official capacity. Shortly after midnight, Cohn-Bendit opened the meeting, recounting the reasons that impelled Nanterre's Culture and Creativity committee to seize the theater: "We must consider this theater, once a symbol of bourgeois and Gaullist culture, now an instrument of combat against the bourgeoisie." He was drowned in uncontrollable enthusiasm and pell-mell. Jean-Louis Barrault followed immediately: "I am in absolute accord with Daniel Cohn-Bendit; Barrault has no interest for history, Barrault is no longer the director of this theater, simply an actor like the others . . . Barrault is dead."[32] In a box seat where, a few weeks prior, a government minister's wife had sat, a worker demanded the floor.

In subsequent weeks, the Odéon experienced a season unequaled in its history, and everyone who was there during its revolutionary "run" came out the better for it. At three in the morning and three in the afternoon every seat was full; lines stood at the entrance waiting to be

---

32. "La culture passe aux acts," *Le Nouvel Observateur,* 20 Mai 1968, p. 8. See also, "Ex-Odéon forum," *Le Monde,* 18 Mai 1968, p. 4.

ushered inside by student monitors. Once within, depending on the audience, one spoke of underdeveloped countries, working conditions, the role of students in class struggle, reason and revolution, the old and the new society.[33]

A La Télévision

Occupation of centers of cultural diffusion by the students represented a logical counterpart to the workers' occupation of their factories. Student intervention in the production of society's intangible goods was a theoretical equivalent to the workers' intervention in production of society's tangible goods. Worker and student, both, felt prisoner of their respective products—a worker by quotas of production, low wages, and little spiritual recompense—a student by a culture in which the student was less the creator than the created. Just as young workers seized factory after factory, demanding self-management, a greater say in policies of production and in the quality of work, so, in parallel fashion, students seized France's system of communication. First the Sorbonne, a temple of learning and house of cultural initiation, then the Odéon Théâtre, the citadel of traditional culture, fell to the movement. There remained mass culture, television and radio still at the service of the Gaullist state—logically the next instrument of cultural diffusion to yield to the revolution.

Television and radio were special cases in France, under firm government control—censorship would be a more appropriate word. This motivated the rumblings heard in the Sorbonne for many days, often at a whisper, regarding direct action against the state television and radio apparatus. While the Odéon passed into its second night of "cultural sabotage," a new expedition was conceived. On Friday morning the students planned to march toward, (and, who knows, possibly invade) the television studios with the support of the workers there: an ideal antidote for the reformist stagnation overtaking the Sorbonne.

The only thing wrong with the idea of this excursion was that it was too bold, for it struck directly at the mainstay of the Gaullist establishment. TV journalists themselves were already talking about striking against government control and, with the addition of a student threat of

---

33. The mood at the Odéon is communicated by "Join the Revolutionary Commune of the Imagination" in the Documents section.

invasion, Pompidou decided to get tough.[34] He arranged a special television broadcast for himself on Thursday evening, May 17, during which he promised to defend the Republic against the disorder that threatened it—that is, against the student radicals.

On top of this, the CGT and Communist Party strongly discouraged their workers from joining in the student demonstrations. Against such odds, student leaders called it off. The demarcation line determining just how far the students could lead a combat on their own had been drawn. Obviously, student power outside the universities was an illusion, and without the major unions and the Communist Party, direct action was impossible. Even before Pompidou's declaration, student leaders seemed to realize that the Sorbonne had played its last trick and that it was now up to the workers to "take from their fragile hands" the revolt that had begun in the Sorbonne.

One had the impression that with the abdication of this demonstration, wild adventures had come to an end. This did not mean surrender, but simply displacement of the energy of revolt. In the National Assembly, left-wing parties combined to propose a Motion of Censure against de Gaulle, to be discussed the next week. Every day new factories closed down. And the struggle for the TV studios was not over, for the students were by no means the only ones concerned with government censorship. On the same day that students decided to abandon their demonstration, radio and television personnel held a meeting to organize a general strike against the mass communication apparatus.

A lack of objectivity and conspicuous omissions on TV news became a notorious scandal during France's national crisis. On May 10, at the tail end of a week of demonstrations, while barricades were being built, the broadcast of "Panorama," a weekly review of events, did not even mention the students. Lack of information? Hardly. Journalists had worked all week, two of them wounded in the process, to assemble films of the demonstrations and gather interviews with Jacques Sauvageot, Alain Geismar, and Nobel Prize professors Monod and Kastler. Shortly before the broadcast, a representative from the Ministry of Education and the Ministry of Information prohibited the program. The next night, at midnight, a censored version of "Panorama" appeared with no account rendered of the famous "night of the barricades." By

---

34. Olivier Oudiette, "ORTF: La grève incomprise," *L'Evènement*, Juillet–Aout 1968, pp. 22–27.

Monday these unreported events would see the whole country closed down by a general strike.

While students certainly resented being slighted on television coverage, it was the journalists who really suffered, having labored to no avail. On Thursday evening, May 16, a spontaneous meeting (by now a familiar phenomenon in the month of May) of journalists decided to call a general assembly for Friday; the following morning, writers, engineers, cameramen, chauffeurs, and even a few directors called a strike, demanding fiscal and political autonomy from the government.

Elsewhere, in the medical school, future doctors organized first-aid crews to service militants in case the fighting continued. A large part of the Sorbonne had been converted into an emergency hospital. The University of Strasbourg declared itself autonomous, provoking similar action from other universities in the provinces. The National School of the Arts declared its talents in the service of the movement and converted its studios into production workshops, printing posters day and night.[35] By Sunday night, one hundred seventy-five action committees met regularly in the neighborhoods.[36] There students and workers gathered to discuss the movement with local residents. A new newspaper called *Action* appeared, representing UNEF, SNEsup, and the March 22 Movement. Feverish activity continued in the schools while, paradoxically, all other national services ground to a halt.

No one worked. No planes, trains, mail. No gas. No trash collection. Neighbors, who had lived within ten feet of each other for twenty years, became acquainted, strolling and talking in the empty streets. So this is a revolution, they said—not bad.

The Government

Compared with the Ex-Théâtre de l'Odéon and with the Sorbonne's critical university, the National Assembly's meetings appeared somewhat dull. Its agendas and discussions lacked the relevancy of these revolutionary forums to France's immediate crisis. At no moment had the student movement made any appeal to a parliamentary political organization, either to participate in a demonstration or translate its demands into legal terms. Whether it was from nonchalance, contempt, or fear of co-optation by professional politicians, there was a truly re-

---

35. See "The People's Studio" in the Documents section.
36. See "Journal of a Neighborhood Action Committee" in the Documents section.

markable distance between the student movement and the parliamentary opposition. As some anonymous sage wrote on the entrance to the Théâtre de l'Odéon: WHEN THE NATIONAL ASSEMBLY BECOMES A BOURGEOIS THEATER, ALL BOURGEOIS THEATERS MUST BECOME NATIONAL ASSEMBLIES.

This inscription turned out to be as prophetic as it was pertinent. Shortly before the National Assembly debate on the Motion of Censure on May 22, cameramen installed their apparatus in the grand hall for the first time in history, and sent the debate into homes of every viewer in the nation. Put suddenly before their constituencies and the nation, the speeches of the deputies bordered more than ever on the inane, and the whole assembly appeared ridiculous. The inscription at the Odéon was realized, for the old theater now served the people, while the people amused themselves by watching the National Assembly.

There should be no confusion between the behavior of the French legislature and that of its executive, for as much as the parliament was ineffective, struggling among contradictory tendencies, the Gaullist executive was united and powerful. Particularly significant was the evolution of Pompidou's attitude toward the crisis, because, barring de Gaulle's sentiments, his weighed most heavily on its outcome. Even though he abhorred the disorder, Pompidou conceded that the student revolt did contain some healthy elements.[37] This view was shared, in fact, by almost everyone in the government, legislative and executive, except those on the very far right, with the remarkable result that almost no one criticized the movement without adding a little self-flagellation for the government's slowness in instituting satisfactory reforms.

Pompidou's views reflected a strong current of French opinion according to which France lagged behind the United States. *Le Defi Americain* by Servan-Schreiber, the most popular book of the year, made just that point. It attracted many readers because it appealed unintentionally to a certain mild anti-Americanism fashionable in de Gaulle's France. In fact, its purpose was not to condemn America at all, but rather France; for its more intelligent readers, it served as an antidote to complacency, showing France what it would take to compete with America. Europe was stalled in a poverty of ideas and talent.[38] The

---

37. "Le débat de l'assemblée Nationale sur les troubles," *Le Monde*, 16 Mai 1968, p. 2.

38. J. J. Servan-Schreiber, "La renaissance de la France," *L'Express*, Supplément Exceptionel, Mai 1968, p. 2.

French university was an especially sad example of the critical lag of "invention." Servan-Schreiber rejoiced in the student revolt, as did many professors and perhaps even Pompidou himself, as the stimulus for a much needed modernization.

This sentiment, quite strong in France, explains the spirit of Pompidou's first reaction to the revolt: to see the student insurrection as a kind of wake-up call that he could use to prove to conservative adversaries that a veritable renaissance was necessary.

But when, at a later stage, the students passed on their radicalism to the workers and the whole affair threatened to become a full-scale revolution, when even the National Assembly got up enough nerve to propose a Motion of Censure, Pompidou found it difficult to make use of the movement for his own ends. He had imagined the renaissance to be a small, administered affair, and his liberalism, accordingly, was of the paternal sort; he wanted to rejoice in the revolt and rule it at the same time.

The massive march on Monday the 13th, directed specifically against de Gaulle, left an open wound in the authority of the state, aggravated by the occupation of Sorbonne and the large response from workers joining the movement. In his presentation to the National Assembly, announcing his first reactions, Pompidou had even then prepared for a possible second phase of the movement. In the same breath in which he had created a blue ribbon committee for reflection on the crisis, he evoked the scarecrow of subversion: "There are individuals, with extensive financial means, connected with an international organization, prepared to fight in the streets, intending to operate subversion in western countries, and especially in Paris at the very moment when this capital has become the arena for the discussion of peace in the Far East."[39] Hand in hand with his desire for reform went his determination to protect his people from a mysterious international conspiracy; if he could not have his tame renaissance, he could still have recourse to a well-justified repression. After the invasion of the Théâtre de l'Odéon, and rumblings of another invasion of the TV studios, Pompidou abandoned the idea of using the movement and treated it as an adversary.

He reckoned, on Thursday evening, that two decisive factors were to his credit: public opinion polls indicated that the student movement, even at its height of popularity, had the support of less than half the French; second, left-wing organizations were in disarray, the moderate

---

39. "Le débat de l'assemblée nationale sur les troubles," op. cit., p. 2.

Federation of the Left reluctant to align with the Communists and the Communists in full campaign against the students. He designed his strategy accordingly: to erect a specter of subversion around all forces of the left, to isolate and divide them, while uniting the rest of the French population in fear. Appearing on a national broadcast Thursday night, he gave a brief, cold speech of defiance of "those who threaten to spread disorder and destroy the nation."

Caught on the one hand between Pompidou's two-faced initiative, a semi-liberal promise and a harsh authoritarian threat, and on the other hand the students' anti-parliamentary attitude, the parties of the left seemed doomed to founder in the National Assembly. Their only hope was to coalesce their strength in the Assembly with centrist support for a Motion of Censure, and to wedge, thereby, a parliamentary power between de Gaulle and the Sorbonne.

On May 22, when France was thoroughly mired down in its paralysis, with not even a vague idea of how the crisis would end, the Assembly opened debate on the motion. By all rights, the Communist Party should have been having its heyday. Ten million workers, its theoretical constituency, had revolted in a mass wave of strikes and paralyzed the nation. But the Party had purposely alienated itself from the revolutionaries to protect its democratic reputation and its very respectable 22 percent of the vote. The Federation of the Left, the major parliamentary opposition to de Gaulle, had in fact considered the Communists respectable enough to solicit an alliance with them in February 1968. Together, they occupied close to half of the Assembly seats and constantly harassed the Gaullists.

Their customary adversaries included a centrist coalition under a clever leader, Giscard d'Estaing, who opposed de Gaulle from the moderate right and was later to be his successor. By May 22, on the eve of the vote on the motion, the only votes unaccounted for were those of d'Estaing. Had his coalition voted against de Gaulle, there would have been no more General. As it was, his crucial block went against the motion and it failed by a margin of eleven votes.

For de Gaulle and Pompidou, his dauphin, this success was tantamount to a mandate for wielding a bigger and heavier stick against the movement. On the morrow of their victory, May 23, the Council of Ministers, drunk with their new confidence, on learning that Cohn-Bendit had temporarily left French territory, made public an order prohibiting his reentry. For this they would answer in the following days.

This flurry of activity around the motion of censure served as comic relief, as the inscription at Odéon artfully foretold. For the moment, the motion's defeat, predictable in advance, solved nothing; it merely created a base for Pompidou and de Gaulle to face a movement that had, even then, not reached its peak.

Triangle of Contention

For two days after the failure of the motion of censure the entire political process stopped, pausing for de Gaulle to deliver his long awaited address to the nation. Speculation suggested that he would call for a national referendum for or against his continued stay in office, based on a promise like that of Pompidou to initiate reforms. So far the tactic of the government, faced with the growing crisis, had changed very little following reaffirmation by the National Assembly. It still offered the students various minor concessions and promised satisfaction of a number of workers' economic demands. Meanwhile, as before, de Gaulle's cabinet continued to brandish the threat of communism and subversion from unknown sources to incite popular fear. Astonishingly, the government seemed to believe itself on top of the crisis.

Seen from the point of view of normality, France painted a very grim picture, so much so that only self-deception or bravado could account for the government's show of confidence. A quick look at France's decomposition sufficed to render account of its extent. Each day another element of the economy closed up. Banks in many parts of the country limited amounts of withdrawals. Television and radio reduced their broadcasts to a bare minimum. Electricity, generated in worker-controlled power plants, blinked on and off to remind the people that the wires were working for the revolution. All national and international communication and transportation had stopped; the national library had jokingly placed a sign on its door saying that the nation no longer needed history. Cinemas and theaters closed down. In Cannes, following the spectacular exit of François Truffaut, the famous film festival entered into the struggle against de Gaulle, protesting censorship in the name of free cinema.[40] Farmers too, if originally reluctant, soon declared their solidarity with students and workers through their various organizations, in some places offering loads of free vegetables to the strikers.

Idlers in the street felt they knew something that the government did not know—that France was in the midst of a national crisis. No assurance from the government could hide this fact. Everyone spoke by way of comparison of the memorable days of 1936, the only time in

---

40. "Cannes en Panne," *Le Nouvel Observateur*, Numéro Special, 20 Mai 1968, p. 8.

recent history that equaled the present moment, when workers had spontaneously occupied their factories often without union orders. Then, a socialist government had befriended the workers, resulting in benefits such as paid vacations unheard of in France before that time. By all rights, the workers and their unions had reason to relish, as they did in 1936, the prospect of the negotiations with management and government planned for the coming weekend.

But in reality the workers' condition and particularly the bargaining position of the unions in 1968 was more different than similar to 1936. It was an irony of history that the workers of 1936 had posed purely quantitative demands with extensive means at their disposal (a single union and a socialist government) while the worker of 1968 found himself posing more *extensive demands* than in 1936, including political demands within and without the factory, with *less means* (four unions divided among themselves, and an extremely unsympathetic government).

What is further revealing about the comparison is the unprecedented role of the student catalyst in 1968. In the first days the students set the tone, demanding political solutions, contemptuous of purely economic demands, providing a model and example of revolutionary defiance, and encouraging the workers to share their optimistic abandon. In sum, while prospects for settlement by arbitration seemed slighter in 1968, those of national revolution appeared greater. This situation held a special significance for the status of the unions, their corporate capacity to bargain, and their conduct—particularly that of the General Confederation of Workers (CGT).

Although associated with the Communist Party, the CGT belonged to a long line of conservative French unionism. The predominance of the CGT in the labor movement had meant the death of a very different French union tradition known as "syndicalism," an anarchist tendency that pursued political insurrection as the ultimate objective of every strike. Remaining the same as ever in 1968, even down to its 74-year-old president who had signed the Matignon Accords of 1936, the CGT now found itself confronted by its historical alternative, and, of all things, coming from the university. The students had resurrected the specter of anarchism in calling for a revolutionary strike.[41]

---

41. *Le Monde* carried extensive commentary on the reactions of the labor unions to the student vanguard. See, in particular, "La prise de position de la CGT, et l'extension du mouvement de grèves," *Le Monde*, 19–20 Mai 1968, pp. 2–3.

The more the students nagged at the flank of the CGT, the more the CGT became rigid and suspicious. The image of Cohn-Bendit at the front of the march of May 13, relishing what he openly called the "Stalinist creeps in tow," set off the conflict. Afterward, George Séguy, Secretary General of the CGT, admonished his workers against fraternizing with the students and strongly discouraged the student march to the Renault factory on Thursday. The CGT refused to support the student demonstration in front of the radio and TV station, and distributed leaflets among workers calculated to arouse suspicion of Sorbonne radicals. The result was that many workers who were sympathetic with the students, particularly with the alternative they posed, having found no representation in the CGT, turned to the French Democratic Confederation of Workers (CFDT), France's second major union and eager rival to the CGT.

Contrary to the CGT, the CFDT immediately perceived the significance of the student movement. Although not as large as the CGT, the CFDT was more flexible and capable of wielding considerable influence in 1968 for two reasons. First, whereas the CGT was aligned with the Communist Party, the CFDT was closer to the Unified Socialist Party (PSU), a small but respectable leftist organization that supported the movement. It escaped the predicament of the CGT Communists, of trying to be respectable while identifying with a revolutionary tradition and not accomplishing either convincingly. Second, since the 1950s it had supported the demand for "union power," which coincided closely with the demands for structural and political changes advocated by the student-worker alliance.

By the third week of May, a triangle of discord on the role of labor in the movement threatened to impede the progress of negotiations: many *young* workers refused all unionism and claimed that negotiations would only make sense after the working class had acquired a position of force independent of the unions. They saw a detonator and model for their own actions in the student movement. The CGT refused to acknowledge the notion of "workers' power" while the CFDT advocated "union power" if not "workers' power," and served as mediator between the CGT and the young workers.

In the week prior to Saturday's negotiations, the meetings among the major unions were strained. On Tuesday, the CFDT repeated its desire "to see the movement maintain itself and develop along the lines of the democratization of industry, including greater participation and self-management." The CGT replied, "The movement can only be hindered by empty formulas such as self-management, reform of civiliza-

49

tion and other inventions which confuse our immediate demands." On Wednesday, the CFDT proposed that "union power in industry parallel that of the students who struggle for university reform, a true democratization of education that the CFDT has supported for many years." On the same day, the CGT declined to meet with student leaders, saying, "UNEF has had the incredible pretension to speak of workers' struggle, and workers' objectives. In these conditions, the CGT considers the meeting with UNEF to hold no interest for either party."

At the end of the week, the CGT began to suspect that it would pay for its alienation of the revolutionaries. One of its most prestigious members resigned in protest of its moderation, and others followed. Soon, it had to defend itself against a wave of accusations that it was in collusion with the government to quietly arrange a quick resolution of the crisis.

Finally on Thursday, May 23, faced with the necessity of presenting concerted demands, the CGT and CFDT reached an accord and, for what it was worth, the CFDT managed to get union liberties in the factories placed at the top of the dossier. Two angles of the triangle of contention appeared temporarily reconciled, but no accord could have been less promising.

Friday Red III

To stay at the Sorbonne in this third week of May was to experience a painful isolation. Once a catalyst and now a symbol of the movement, the Sorbonne was considered more folklore than focus. Originally, the students had isolated themselves from the major leftist organizations to preserve their initiative in the hopes that the movement would eventually overwhelm prudent tradition with their own style of radicalism. Begun with the greatest audacity and confidence in their audience, the scheme backfired later in the month and left the Sorbonne with only the audacity, and no audience among the major parties of the left.[42]

Stagnation and bitter isolation had reached a peak when the Counsel of Ministers, arrogant with the defeat of the Motion of Censure, issued an order against Cohn-Bendit's reentry into France.[43] In its very attempt to dismantle the bomb of the student movement, the govern-

---

42. "M. Séguy écarte dans l'immédiate l'éventualité d'un ordre de grève générale illimitée," *Le Monde,* 19–20 Mai 1968, p. 2.

43. Although a long-time resident of France, Cohn-Bendit was a German citizen. Today he is a political leader in the German Green Party.

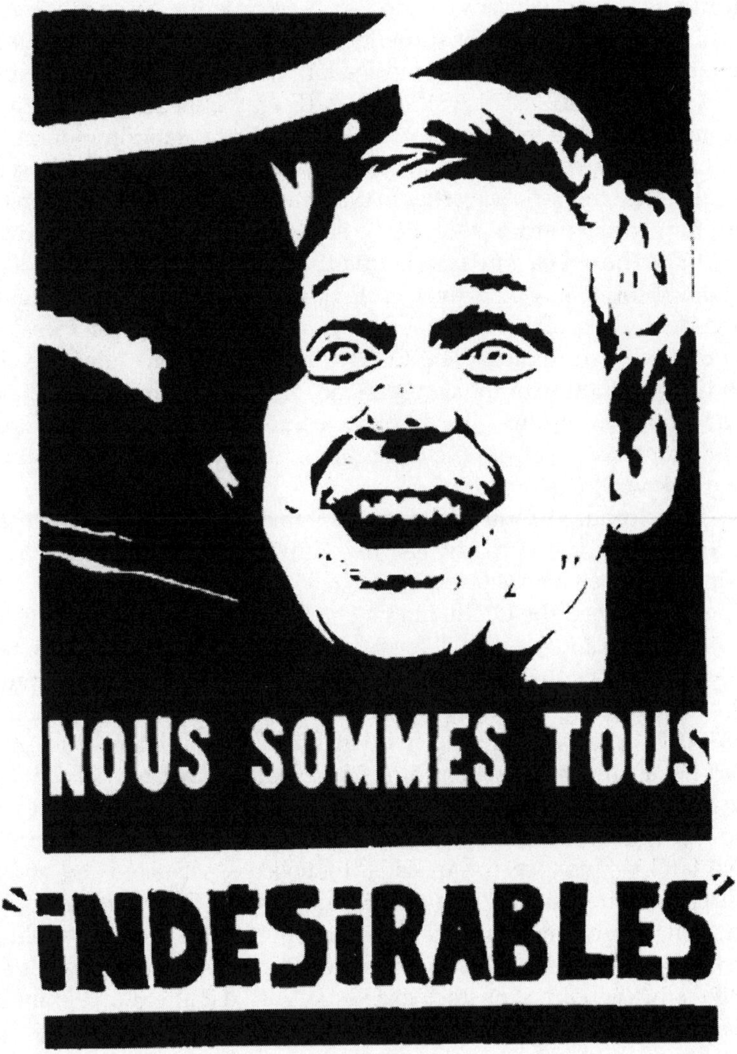
NOUS SOMMES TOUS
"INDÉSIRABLES"

ment had unwittingly done the opposite; it had provided the remedy for the stagnation of the Sorbonne by once again lighting the fuse.

Simultaneous with the announcement, a tremor of anger passed through the diffused conversation at the Sorbonne. Reaction was instinctive, and thousands of students descended into the Latin Quarter, identifying with their forbidden leader, Cohn-Bendit. They shouted, WE ARE ALL GERMAN JEWS, WE ARE ALL FOREIGNERS, sensing intuitively that the machinery of revolt was once again in motion. The familiar pattern too was once again repeated as a few groups refused to abandon the streets on the order to disperse, and violent combat ensued until four in the morning.

Onto the streets of Paris poured three demonstrations the following day. Students, called by UNEF and marching in protest against Cohn-Bendit's prohibition, emerged a determined lot from weeks of struggle with the police. The CGT called a march to reinforce their failing reputation with the workers and show their strength on the eve of negotiations. From a third corner came the farmers, traditionally anti-communist, yet from the beginning of the week tending more and more to favor the students.

Two hundred thousand farmers surrounded the city with their tractors, blocking the roadways; five hundred thousand came to the CGT march between 4:00 P.M. and 6:00 P.M., many of whom, after dispersing, joined the UNEF march at 8:00 P.M. when a countless number of student and worker demonstrators assembled around the Gare de Lyon. At this hour, General de Gaulle prepared to address the nation.

Almost everyone expected some kind of surprise, at least some well-turned phrases from the General, after his customary fashion. Instead his address was seven minutes of bland reiteration of what the press had predicted for four days: a call for a referendum on his leadership and some extremely vague promises for reform.[44] Even before the termination of his speech, barricades had been constructed and a car set on fire. From the Gare de Lyon, two groups formed. One marched toward City Hall to threaten a historical repetition of its seizure in the revolution of 1871.[45] The other headed down darkened streets toward the citadel of capitalism, the Bourse, or stock exchange, with the intention of ransacking and burning the building. Surely no one expected capitalism to die in the flames, but it seemed an appropriately symbolic act.

---

44. "L'Allocution du chef de l'état," Le Monde, 26–27 Mai 1968, p. 2.
45. The Commune of Paris began with a seige of the City Hall.

The mood of these marchers grew increasingly somber as they approached the financial center of French capitalism. Young men broke into construction sites along the way and equipped themselves with workers' helmets and wooden sticks. Halfway, the march divided into two separate columns, the better to evade any police barriers that might be ahead. Soon afterward, one of those columns found itself walking toward a T intersection. The end of the street was blocked by a large public building and those at the head of the crowd turned to the left under its facade.

Suddenly the word came down through the long column as one row after another hissed "Shhh, shhh" to those behind. Wondering why, the marchers fell absolutely silent and walked on tiptoes toward the building at the end of the street. As they approached, they saw the reason. A large sign read: "Quiet. Hospital Zone."

Are real revolutionaries courteous? A strange courtesy in any case, which did not prevent the marchers from setting fire to the Bourse briefly afterwards, before turning south toward familiar territory in the Latin Quarter where a battle raged till dawn.

Where Rue Monsieur le Prince joins the Boulevard St. Michel, one hundred and fifty students, fitted out with helmets, handkerchiefs, and garbage can lids for shields, formed chains of labor; some wrenched stones from the pavement and passed them along to a joyous crowd pushed up against a sprouting barricade of rocks, cement blocks, and piles of crates on trees and cars. Every barricade took an immense effort.

Then an assault would begin, with a wave of tear gas and minor explosives as a warning. The air became thick, unbreathable, impenetrable, and the barricade faded from view in a cloud of gas. So did its makers, who scampered around corners while their masterpiece, their imitation of defense, was overrun in an instant.

The barricade was an anomaly. Except for rare instances it protected no one, for by the time the CRS had arrived, there was no one there. No more than a haphazard pile of rock and debris, it served to impede the advance of the enemy only a single second where an hour was needed. An observer, taking shelter in an alleyway, was struck by this absurdity: what are you pretending for? While you make paper fortresses, the police beat down on you like rats; better to be a mercenary and fight, than a visionary building imaginary barricades. Burn the town down if you don't like how it's run. A red flag is no defense against a bull. What is the meaning of this half-scale war? Is it not to court despair and forget about victory? Take a lesson from the riots of

American/Blacks—rape the whole society, break its precious store windows, steal its goods, the gods of its complacent consumer.

On this Friday, May 24, as violence raged, a band of ruffians saw their chance to profit from the lack of law and order; fifteen of them ravaged a store window and jauntily strolled away with their loot. In a few instants a circle formed around them until a band of student monitors came at a run, seized the loot, replaced it in the store window, and left marks of reprimand on the guilty.

Violence was symbolic and not irresponsibly destructive. Student leaders were constantly accused of being professional agitators, urban guerillas with no ideals, leading childish masses with a passion for disorder. This they were not. Impassioned, yes, but visionaries and not looters, using disorder to the end of a new order. Violence was simply communication, a sign language directed toward a state that refused to listen to words. This revolution had no respect for law, but it was sophisticated enough to distinguish between individual criminality and collective political action. There may have been deaths but murders were impossible. The violence of May was neither abhorrent nor absurd.

De Gaulle or Not de Gaulle

It is a macabre Saturday morning in the Latin Quarter. A mopping-up operation scatters the few remaining demonstrators into a somber rain. Onto the steps of the Théâtre de l'Odéon, a recognized neutral location, some students gather around a radio in despair. An announcer makes light of the last skirmishes of fatigued resistance; like de Gaulle's speech the night before, his commentary seems farcical and ignoble.

De Gaulle's speech had been the most painful: focusing the crisis around his own person, with a promise of reforms based on the vague idea of "participation." A verbal panacea for all social ills, de Gaulle's participation appeared irrelevant to the grievances that had given rise to revolt. IF THE PEOPLE VOTE NO, de Gaulle had concluded, he would no longer fulfill the functions of his office. But IF BY A MASSIVE YES the people returned him their confidence, he would, as many times before, take in hand the necessary changes. Even his own party did not like the idea of his tagging himself as the price of order, or relying on his own paternal power to subdue a nation of children. Why had he waited so long to remedy the crisis, and then virtually deny it by telling his people that, if they trusted in him, things would be all right?

The balance of power had begun to shift away from de Gaulle, though the direction of the shift seemed impossible to determine. After twenty-one days of procrastination, his address, notable mainly for a conspicuous lack of any serious promise of change, opened a credibility gap that he had always been able to fill before by force of his personality or political cleverness.

PART III. THE LAST ACT

Workers versus Negotiations

Although of questionable solidity, there existed for the first time in many years an accord between the two major unions, the General Confederation of Workers (CGT) and the French Democratic Confederation of Workers (CFDT). As the mass of workers came more and more to sympathize with the students and the CFDT, the CGT found itself drawn against its will into the radicalization process. The resulting alliance was far from being natural or permanent; nevertheless, it had produced for Saturday afternoon a common front long unknown among the unions in France.

Opening on Saturday afternoon, negotiations right away struck an optimistic note as the government accepted the unions' proposition for a huge minimum wage increase. But on Sunday this hope disappeared. Bargaining was almost impossible. A crucial moment came when the electricians of the CFDT demanded an immense raise of 20 percent and briefly interrupted city-wide current to show they meant it. On into Sunday night, the representatives hardened their positions, promising a long and difficult session.

Much to everyone's surprise, at the turn of midnight on Sunday, following a private meeting between Pompidou and a CGT official, Pompidou predicted that negotiations would be finished by morning. And, sure enough, a settlement, known as the Protocol of Grenelle, was released Monday morning.[46]

But when the union leaders took their package to the workers, not a single factory accepted the settlement or resumed work. Either the unions had misjudged the sentiment of the workers or the CGT had deliberately ignored it with some obscure strategy in mind. In any case, the insufficiency of the settlement and the subsequent massive rejection gave a second wind to the strikes. Now the tone of the workers' movement assumed a decidedly political character, particularly at Renault,

---

46. "Le protocole d'accord entre les syndicats," *Le Monde,* 28 Mai 1968, p. 1.

where CGT President, Benoît Frachon, tried unsuccessfully to convince young workers to resume work.

Instead of shouts of joy over the settlement, the CGT encountered boos and hisses. Frachon was followed to the dais by André Jeanson, his counterpart in the CFDT. Jeanson profited from the situation, putting his smaller union in a good light by responding to the temper of the gathering. Jeanson began his speech by congratulating the workers for their refusal to end the strike:

> I hope that other factories are doing the same thing at this time. To make the government and the bosses accept a 30% raise in the SMIG [minimum wage for industry] and a 10% wage increase is already a victory for us, but it is only a step. We are fighting for democracy in the factories to put an end to the monarchy of the bosses. We rejoin the student and teacher movement. Our actions converge.[47]

Tangible demands had proved a liability to the CGT. The intangible notion of democratization, now adopted by the workers, gave rise to a concept of a new society, unclear as yet, but inscribed in the enthusiastic revolutionism of the CFDT and the student movement. Meanwhile the CGT and its political counterpart, the Communist Party, found themselves outstripped by their more aggressive rivals and this time they felt it. A metamorphosis began to occur in these two organizations, toward a more clearly defined refusal of de Gaulle and a greater acceptance of the vague idea of self-management. The Communists sent out an urgent request to the Federation of the Left to set up a political program, and the CGT called twelve meetings around the city to explain their new strategy.

The Gaullist Gap

De Gaulle's failure to pacify the revolutionaries, and the Communists' failure to absorb them, created a vacuum of political direction in the last days of May. Into this gap rushed a host of aspirants. The student-worker alliance, including the United Socialist Party (PSU) and the CFDT, met to establish a political union beyond the barricades. The Federation of the Left, previously reluctant to venture into a fluctuating

---

47. Ibid., p. 1.

situation, now took its cue: Mitterand, its chief, proposed a provisional government of the left, anticipating the absence of de Gaulle after the referendum. Mendès-France, a singular political figure in France, made his own private attempt to co-opt the student-worker movement and came closer than anybody to succeeding.[48]

For one memorable afternoon, everyone on the same side of the barricades found themselves on the same side of the political fence. UNEF called a demonstration for Monday, May 27, which was joined by the CFDT and PSU, in addition to the customary conglomeration of student and professor groups that made up the majority of the movement. Most sensational of all were the latest adherents to the movement, discontents and deserters from the CGT and Communist Party, of whom the most famous was André Barjonet, ex-high union leader. Marching to the large Charléty stadium, they experienced a temporary wave of solidarity, generated partly in common opposition to the Communist Party, which had refused to condone the congregation at Charléty, and partly in further defiance of de Gaulle's government, which had threatened to forcibly prevent it. After a long series of speakers, André Barjonet, defector from the CGT, approached the platform to a roar of acclaim. Barjonet was, for the moment, the last best hope for a radical political alliance: "Today the revolution is possible. If I quit the CGT it is because the leaders did not know or did not want to know that the present situation is truly revolutionary. It is necessary to organize and organize fast."

Meanwhile, those who had waited impatiently for Mitterand's press conference on Tuesday afternoon were not in the least disappointed. He bet everything on the failure of the referendum, took his risks, and jumped into the gulf of "after-de Gaulle-what?" He proposed the following: preparation of a provisional government competent to serve as a fair arbitrator for students and workers, and to organize presidential elections. Thus, the heavy machinery of the French political left, slow getting started, was finally set in motion.

Mendès-France, in contrast to Mitterand, had always been a tactful, reserved man, the man Mitterand needed, but who did not particularly need Mitterand. One-time president of the Council of Ministers, he knew perhaps better than anyone the many obstacles in the way of an

---

48. Mendès-France was widely respected in France as a talented and honest political leader. As premier under the Fourth Republic, he disengaged France from its Indochina war.

ambitious politician in France. Wisely, he kept a skillful distance from the big battalions of the left, while making appearances at opportune times and places. On May 23, he had ventured down into the Latin Quarter, during a night of barricades and protest for Cohn-Bendit, and he also followed the demonstration to Charléty, where he offered his silent assent to the movement. Only after Mitterand's press conference did he prepare to re-enter the heavy atmosphere of the parliamentary left, announcing his own conference on the next day.

Wednesday, May 29, was full of suspense; de Gaulle had mysteriously left the Elysée Palace shortly before his weekly cabinet meeting, for a place unknown, and there were rumors that he would resign. The CGT planned a demonstration on Wednesday which rallied close to 500,000 participants, and this time, joined by the Communist Party, they called for a popular front government. Into this political soup went Mendès-France as well, with the full support of the CFDT and eventually that of Mitterand, announcing that he would accept leadership in a provisional government.

With each day that passed in this last week of May, a great excitement spread from student activists to union leaders to politicians and idlers as the movement advanced closer and closer to the sources of power, farther from its isolation, farther from its moment of discouragement, bending Communism to revolution, pulling its amorphous mass into a coherent force for change.

CGT and Communists Re-Revolutionize

The Communist-CGT block felt more painfully than ever a victim of circumstances. Normally the most outspoken critics of all, lately they had spent more time denying accusations than making them. While the Gaullists accused them of starting the revolution, at Charlét the student-worker/PSU-CFDT alliance accused them of betraying the movement.

Between Monday and Wednesday, a striking change took place in the CGT and the Communist Party, noticeable in the more severe tone of the CGT following its twelve meetings throughout Paris on Monday evening. It was noticeable also in a peculiar exchange between the CGT and UNEF on Tuesday afternoon. It seemed that the CGT all of a sudden wished to make peace with the students and asked UNEF to join its march on Wednesday. For some reason, not comprehensible to anyone, UNEF refused to participate.

This change in the communist position took place primarily because more than ever before a real crisis seemed pending. France was a mess by Wednesday afternoon. Pompidou had pleaded with the workers to vote on the return to work by secret ballot but they refused. Discussion on the return to work in public facilities like the railways and subways had not even begun. In the mining regions of the North, CGT leaders had already declared that their factories would not resume work without a popular front government. There had been no gas in Paris for a week, no mail for two weeks, electricity went on and off, and people were getting worried. Pompidou was supposed to have asked de Gaulle to retire, and if there could be anything worse than Gaullism for most of the French, it was post-Gaullism.

Five hundred thousand workers and a few students marched in the CGT's metamorphosis march. From the Place de la Bastille to the Gare St. Lazare, the demonstration planned to pass audaciously close to de Gaulle's Elysée Palace where the police were prepared for an invasion. This time, the slogans did not demand increased salaries or a forty hour week as on the previous Friday, but rather a *Gouvernement Populaire* and de Gaulle's resignation.

The Return of Cohn-Bendit

Once again the Sorbonne is in tumult. The only resemblance to democracy is that everyone is equally inaudible. The FER (Federation of Revolutionary Students) says student power must make itself known to the factories; the JCR (Young Communist Revolutionaries) says the movement must go back into the streets. The UJCML (Union of Marxist-Leninist Communist Youth) objects to both of them; the March 22 Movement claims that UNEF is an undercover agent for the government, and fights break out on the floor of the Grand Amphitheatre.

In a corner of the entrance hall, a curled up student monitor snores uncomfortably, while another plays the guitar. It is now almost ten o'clock and for this one moment calm has returned; the next moment a comrade runs from a side door and rushes from behind the platform, "Comrades, I think now we can talk politics seriously with a comrade who will take the floor after me." Behind him stands a rather heavyset, slightly comical brown-haired character: "Our comrade, Cohn-Bendit!"

A moment of stupor and murmuring. After two weeks in the Sorbonne, very few conversations receive the attention of the audience behind the first few rows where participants usually argue among themselves. As the word spreads, incredulous eyes search for this antihero; someone runs outside to awaken the stretched-out monitor and alert the guitar player, who continues to scratch at his instrument as incredulous as the others.

He had returned that night, loose, confident, cool, his hair dyed, as he reported, by a "marvelous young girl." "I walked through the woods from Germany into France," he further explained, "listened to the birds singing, then took a comfortable car to Paris. Anyone who wants can enter France with a revolutionary organization behind them." He reiterated his favorite themes: "The meeting at Charléty was fine, but it is necessary to organize further. We must avoid getting bogged down in theory and ideology; otherwise, in two weeks, Mitterand, the unions and the government will arrive at a solution suitable to them all, and the movement will be smothered. An organization is possible—simply witness what we have so far created—a revolutionary movement in a modern capitalist country, something unique in the world."

No one would have predicted at this moment that the movement was rushing toward its end. No one would have had the perspective to see in France anything other than occupied factories, angry students, and ambitious politicians, though indeed, while most of France had been paralyzed, it had not been convinced. On the eve of May 30, an ill omen appeared: for the first time in a week and a half, picket lines allowed gas trucks to enter and lines of replenished cars filed out of Paris carting loads of anxious Parisians into the countryside from where they hoped to watch this dirty business of revolution cleaned up by the General.

The End of May

Among those nonrevolutionaries who did not scamper from the scene of disruption, a countermovement began which, on Thursday the 30th of May, came forward in an impressively large demonstration for de Gaulle. These were the people who believed Pompidou's scarecrow of subversion, along with Fouchet's caricature of the movement as led by gangsters and criminals. Their rhetoric had succeeded in driving away from the movement all those middle-of-the-road politicians who did not want to taint their reputation with a subversive cause. It rallied, at the same time, various normally divided right-wing publics that coalesced in opposition to the subversives and joined the Gaullist demonstration on Thursday afternoon.

The turning point was not reached, however, before de Gaulle had a last and serious scare that came close to provoking his resignation. For government ministers, the metamorphosis within the Communist Party and the CGT was grave news. They had been comforted since the beginning of the factory occupations that the Party and the CGT had expressed no insurrectional ambitions. After the workers rejected the *Protocol de Grenelle,* and these two organizations obviously no longer controlled their own troops, the ministers could only prepare for the worst. The Party and the CGT could not be expected to abandon their members, nor continue to oppose them. The only alternative these organizations had left was to match their passion. This they had begun to do on Monday, at the CGT's twelve meetings, which were followed by Tuesday's appeal to the students for a reconciliation, and finally with Wednesday's march, planned to pass dangerously close to de Gaulle's abode.

By this time, the ministers had panicked. Pompidou himself attempted to get de Gaulle to resign. A distinguished group of veteran Gaullists addressed a letter to the president suggesting resignation. In the evening, the president received his generals and gave a series of orders. Secret documents of the Elysée, along with de Gaulle's family, were hurried off and put in their respective safe places.

On Wednesday morning, when his cabinet ministers arrived for the scheduled meeting, President de Gaulle was absent; the meeting had been delayed for a day, and an Elysée official revealed that he had left for his home in Colombey for a brief stay. Would he retire? Or would he return with his troops, rumored since early morning to be marching toward Paris?

Early Wednesday morning, the French Ambassador informed the German Chancellor, Willy Brandt, that de Gaulle would pass through Germany later in the day to visit his major military installations. It was there that the General confirmed the continued support of his army officers.

Meanwhile, tension mounted in Paris on Thursday. The radio announced that de Gaulle would give a speech at 3:00 P.M., and what with the future of the movement and the future of France at stake, this speech, his second major commentary during the events, would necessarily be of historical moment. By 3:00 P.M. the Gaullist demonstration had reached huge proportions, filling the Place de la Concorde, waving tricolor flags, coining a few phrases of its own: THE REVOLUTION WITH DE GAULLE, COHN-BENDIT TO DACHAU. On the left bank, little groups coagulated around a radio to hear the General.

"In the circumstances," he began, "I will not resign. I have my duty to the people, I will fulfill it." Word by word his tone hardened. He dissolved the National Assembly, and called for legislative elections instead of a presidential referendum, putting off the referendum until a later date. France must not be threatened, he concluded with firm and cold resolve, by: "Intimidation, propaganda and tyranny exercised by groups organized for these expressed purposes, a threat which is in fact a totalitarian enterprise. If this situation continues, I will have to take measures provided by the constitution, other than immediate elections, in order to maintain the Republic. France is menaced by a dictatorship. It is subject to constraint and to the imposition of a power produced in national despair, that is, that of totalitarian communism."

A wave of consternation swept through groups of left-bank critics. De Gaulle had not resigned, but had declared his own counterrevolution, and he was not alone. The Gaullist demonstration left the Place de la Concorde triumphantly, heading up the Champs Elysées along the same path that the students had followed on Tuesday, May 7. It arrived at the Tomb of the Unknown Soldier, and there under the Arc de Triomphe, the chords of the *Marseillaise* wafted in the air amid a crowd of hundreds of thousands.

One wonders exactly what went through de Gaulle's thoughts in the course of these few days when his regime, a regime built largely on his own person, threatened to crumble. Many credible sources reported that, in fact, he had thought about resigning and his generals dissuaded him. The only other reasonable alternative was to declare full-scale war on the movement, which he did; it was not a time for moderation, and once having assured himself of support from the army he pushed all the buttons. The destiny of France was not so easily going to escape the even grander destiny of the man, de Gaulle, the man who represented himself in a television program of June 7 as a "solitary angel" saving the multitude from "totalitarian devils." The spirit of a nation was still that of a single man.

He had proposed in fact the very same thing as had Mitterand and Mendès-France, the Communists, and others who had entered the political arena: that is, dissolution of the National Assembly and national elections. Except there was a twist, a Gaullist twist: de Gaulle was not going to resign, and the elections were going to be conducted according to his own interpretation of the national situation. He left no room for political compromise; the people had to choose between totalitarian communism and "La France"—in other words between violence and submission. This left Mitterand, Mendès-France, and other moderate left-wingers squeezed in between revolution and reaction, and out of the political race.

The question of reforms seldom figured strongly in the three-week electoral campaign—it was either de Gaulle or revolution. Naturally, some anti-Gaullist aspirants banked their whole program on reforms, but the Gaullist gap no longer existed. It had snapped shut and anyone who had stepped into the political arena had to face not only a masterful political opponent, but a father image who had promised to protect his people against a mysterious danger. So, the elections amounted to little more than a three-week poster campaign and a few television appearances during which time the ranks of the revolutionaries were scattered. Many students left for vacation as the Gaullist electoral machine swung into motion, and once more the economy began to turn, lulling people back into day-to-day normalcy.

Little by little the revolt and revolters subsided. The Communist Party tried to recover its previous moderate image for the upcoming national elections. The CGT returned to convincing the workers that the Grenelle agreement was not so bad after all, even though the strikes continued well into June. When the police intervened in a branch of Renault outside of Paris at Flins a new upheaval threatened, though it lacked the massive support that accompanied earlier demonstrations.[49] The same was true for the last student uprising that threatened on June 10, after the drowning of a young demonstrator fleeing from the police. Boulevard St. Michel once more served as the scene of a battle; fifteen hundred arrested, seventy-two barricades, five police stations attacked. But by this time, even though the students were experienced, the police were even more so and they charged with a killing brutality.

On June 11, the government banned all radical leftist organizations; on the 14th, police re-seized and evacuated the Théâtre de l'Odéon. On the 16th, under pretense of the presence of "subversive elements," the police seized and evacuated the university as well. Television and radio personnel still struggled, but differences among them prevented them from gaining the autonomy they desired.

And then the elections, June 23 and 30: victory for de Gaulle. Gaullist deputies took 358 of the 485 seats in the national assembly, gaining ninety-seven seats since the last elections. The Federation of the Left lost sixty-one seats and the Communist Party, thirty-nine. A final blow was reported toward the end of election—Mendès-France himself failed to regain his seat from his district in Grenoble by a margin of 122 votes.

---

49. See "The Students at Flins" in the Documents section.

Where was the revolution of yesterday? Publications filled the stores taking the movement out of the streets and putting it into print. On July 14, Bastille Day, de Gaulle marched victoriously up the Champs Elysées, performing his yearly function and recounting, as always, the struggle of past wars. In the Latin Quarter a young man hawked a new magazine of revolutionary humor and information: LEARN TO BUILD THE BARRICADE. SOUVENIRS, PICTURES, COBBLESTONES. LEARN TO BUILD THE BARRICADE. . . .

The Aftermath

In the wake of failed revolutions, the banality of everyday politics resumes. So it was in France. Although thousands of revolutionaries, including many who quit the Communist Party in disgust, struggled to build a new revolutionary organization to continue the movement, they were ultimately unsuccessful. De Gaulle, his power reaffirmed, attempted to co-opt as much of the reformist content of the movement as he could, to use it as a lever for modernizing the society along lines first sketched by Pompidou early in the course of the Events. The Gaullists thus announced that they were the very "Imagination in Power" for which the students had called. One could doubt their sincerity as they initiated the reform of the university by covering the cobblestones of the Latin Quarter with asphalt. Meanwhile, police repression intensified, disbanding organizations, prohibiting publications, and imprisoning activists. The predictable failure of this contradictory experiment led to de Gaulle's fall from power within a year in another referendum. But conditions were different now. The left was divided and discredited. Pompidou was easily elected to replace de Gaulle; the voters wanted reassurance above all.

The Socialist and Communist Party finally agreed in 1972 on a Common Program of Government, which became their platform in succeeding elections. This platform proposed an electoral path toward a new kind of socialism based on public ownership and democratic control of industry, goals vaguely similar to the students' idea of self-management, but in any case distinguishing French socialism clearly from Russian communism. Pompidou was followed in the presidency by Giscard d'Estaing, and finally, in 1981, by Mitterand, representing the left electoral alliance and its Common Program. Mitterand's long rule (he was elected to two seven-year terms) confirmed the worst fears of the activists of 1968. At first he carried out the main provisions of the Common Program by immediately nationalizing most of French indus-

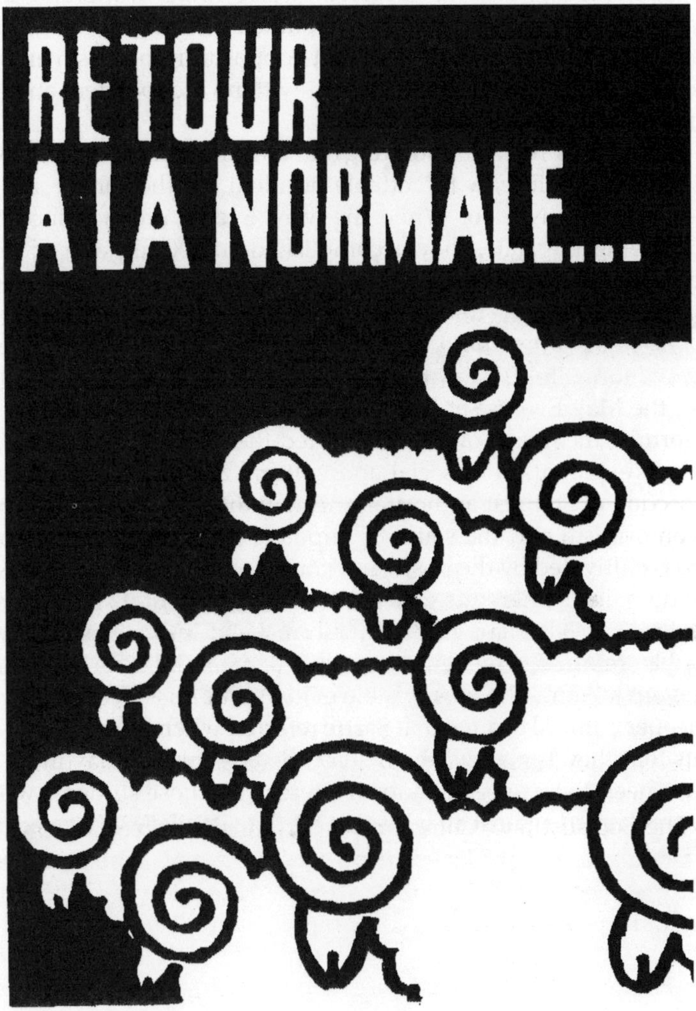
RETOUR
A LA NORMALE...

try, banks, and insurance companies. But as soon as economic problems threatened, he just as quickly privatized the recently nationalized firms and so ended France's final flirtation with socialism. The modernization de Gaulle failed to achieve occurred largely under Mitterand, as the French economy grew by leaps and bounds. The French left has since become a liberal force, admirable in its opposition to racism and willingness to defend the welfare state, but with no independent and original project.

Does this rather disappointing outcome mean that the May Events were an utter failure, a forgettable accident on the long route to a modern France? Not so. While the May Events did not succeed in overthrowing the state, they accomplished something else of importance. They transformed resistance to technocratic authority and consumer society from the notion of a few disgruntled literary intellectuals into a basis for a new kind of mass politics that continues to live in a variety of forms to this day. Like other similar movements around the world, the May Events set in motion a process of cultural change that transformed the image of the left, shifted the focus of opposition from economic exploitation to social and cultural alienation, and prepared the rejection of Stalinist authoritarianism in the new social movements. The conformism and the sense of impotence before the vast forces of progress cultivated by the postwar technocracy gave way to activism in many domains. Ambitious goals formulated in absolute revolutionary terms in the 1960s were gradually retranslated into more modest but realizable reforms. The feminist movement and the environmental movement are only the most visible evidence of this opening. It was to this deeper cultural change that Sartre referred when he said of the May Events that they "enlarged the field of the possible." Today more than ever we need to recover the hope expressed by those students who, in 1968, proclaimed against all odds that "Progress will be what we want it to be."

Two
DOCUMENTS OF
THE MAY MOVEMENT

Commentary and translation by Andrew Feenberg

INTRODUCTION

It was a curious feature of the movement that its motives and goals were not well understood in advance either to actors or commentators. Its *raison d'etre*, its direction and objectives, were elaborated in the course of the Events. Hence, every action was accompanied by a profusion of spoken and written debate. The following documents seek to recreate the course of events, the atmosphere, and the positions taken on critical issues through a selection of leaflets and important articles written during the movement by participants.

This collection is designed to convey something of the mood of the Events by assembling some essential pieces of this debate, allowing influential spokespersons and experiences to speak for themselves. To this end we have made an effort to describe the specific context of each document, its timing, the stance of the authors as well as the circumstances of its dissemination and reception.

The documents also serve to illustrate and support a series of hypotheses about the meaning and significance of the May Events. These hypotheses are presented in brief essays that reconsider the May Events in the light of four central themes: the struggle against technocracy; the ideological crisis of the middle strata; the relations between workers and students; and a new libertarian image of socialism. In challenging both the French government and its official opposition around these themes, the May Events invented a new form of antitechnocratic politics.

This collection is necessarily selective. We have not included many leaflets by *groupuscules* or materials produced by the university reform movement. These are adequately represented in other collections and less interesting than material from the mainstream of the movement.[1] Many of our choices have been drawn from two basic sources: the *Cahiers de Mai* and *Action*. The first was a magazine put out

---

1. See A. Schnapp and P. Vidal-Naquet, *The French Student Uprising* (Boston: Beacon, 1971).

by participants in the movement; its goal was to print short articles on exemplary struggles, preferably written by participants or eyewitnesses. *Action* was the revolutionary student newspaper that appeared daily during much of May and for some time afterward. Both are primary sources for an understanding of the Events.

Essay I. Technocracy and Student Revolt

"Why do they fight? Because they refuse to become the watchdogs of the bourgeoisie."[2]

During the May Events a pamphlet called the "Amnesty of Blinded Eyes" became something of a manifesto of the movement. It began: "There is no student problem. The student is an outdated idea." This leaflet, like many others, claimed that student revolt was not about the situation in the universities. One could observe this same refusal to concentrate on immediate student issues in the American, Chinese, Italian, Mexican, indeed most of the other major student movements of the 1960s.[3] Although changes in the university often formed the background to these revolts, students quickly graduated from demands for university reform to protest in the name of peace and freedom.

Most student movements of the 1960s were defined by solidarity with the oppressed, in whose name they made universal demands. In

---

2. Rather than burdening the remaining text with footnotes to ephemeral documents, I will list here in order the titles of the leaflets and newsletters quoted in this introductory essay. I will follow the same practice in each of the four essays that follow. All translations are mine. "Roche Démission," published in early May 1968, unsigned. "L'Amnistie des Yeux Crevés," May 11, published by Nous Sommes en Marche. Translated in Schnapp and Vidal-Naquet (1971), pp. 448ff. "Continuous la Lutte dans la Rue," Mouvement de 22 Mars, May 12. Graffiti from the walls of Paris during the May Events. A collection of these was published under the title *Les Murs Ont la Parole* (Paris: Tchou, 1968). "Camarades," in Action, no. 1, 7 Mai 1968, p. 4. "Pourquoi Nous Nous Battons," Action no. 1, 7 Mai 1968, p. 4. "L'Amnistie des Yeux Crevés." Ibid.

3. *Daedalus*, Winter, 1968.

the United States the student movement struggled on behalf of blacks and Vietnamese; it can only be understood in the context of the bonds of solidarity, imaginary or real, that linked it to these groups. The French student movement was similarly based on solidarity with workers. The universalism of these movements was particularly surprising in the West, where student revolt supplied a practical refutation of the supposed "end of ideology."

French students were painfully conscious of the significance of such solidarity, given their social destiny within French capitalism. A leaflet of the March 22 Movement states:

> The college and high school students, the young unemployed, the professors and the workers did not fight side by side on the barricades last Saturday to save a university in the exclusive service of the bourgeoisie. This is a whole generation of future executives who refuse to be the planners for the bourgeoisie and agents of the exploitation and repression of the workers.

The language of this leaflet has a deceptively outmoded air. It conjures a long history of French intellectuals placing themselves in the service of the working class through the good offices of the Communist Party. But, as we will see, the French students of 1968 had nothing in common with classical intellectuals motivated by philanthropic concern for the welfare of their social inferiors. In fact, one graffiti on the walls of Paris read: DO NOT SERVE THE PEOPLE. THEY WILL SERVE THEMSELVES. Thus, despite its borrowings from Marxism, the French Communist Party was suspicious of the students and condemned the movement as profoundly alien to its traditions, as indeed it was.

New causes were disguised in the old language of the movement. The rise of technocratic ideology was one of these new causes in the environment of the university that destroyed its inner equilibrium for a time. Student resistance was directed against the growing pressures to achieve a technocratic integration of the university and society. To these pressures on the university there corresponded the dystopian consciousness of the students who hoped to change the system before it became their job to run it.

"Technocracy" means "scientific" management of economic and social affairs. In a technocratic society, the hierarchy of wealth and power is supposed to reflect gradations in ability. No longer does mere wealth or birth justify privilege. Now education and competence have this function. Of course, technocracy is more an ideology than a reality.

In both state socialist and advanced capitalist societies, technocratic administration rationalizes the exercise of power by traditional political and economic elites; in neither does it replace them.[4]

But if technocratic ideology is not altogether true, it is plausible enough and believed enough to change the image of the university, that breeding ground of technical competence. The new university has been called a "knowledge factory," a factory in which knowledge and the knowledgeable are produced.[5] It supplies the technocratic hierarchy with its members and it is also the place in which the new scientific knowledge used by this hierarchy is first discovered. Furthermore, the university is like the society in that it too is divided into the trained and the untrained, the knowledgeable and the ignorant.

There is thus a metaphoric equivalence between society, which professes to be based on knowledge, and the university, which actually is so based. One leaflet comments: "For us the faculty and the student body are only grotesque miniaturizations of social classes, projected onto the university milieu, and this is why we reject the right of the faculty to exist as such." The university could be seen as an idealized model of the society in which differences in knowledge justified different functions and privileges.

Although most French students were poor in 1968, they were predestined to take their place in the hierarchies of business and government after graduation. They could not define themselves in terms of poverty and exploitation, and were in fact seen by workers as incipient oppressors. The only significant resemblance between workers and students was their lack of qualifications. In any other society, this particular equation between workers and students would be irrelevant, but in a society dominated by technocratic ideology, in which all forms of subordination are explained and justified in terms of levels of expertise, students could be said to suffer in its purest and most abstract form the same domination as workers.

At least in their own sphere, students were aware of the immediate relation between gratuitous bureaucratic authority and their own powerlessness. They knew that many of the pretensions of the society were fraudulent as they applied to the university, and that the educational bureaucracy was not only undemocratic, but profoundly incom-

---

4. The theme of technocracy was a central one for commentators on May 1968. Alain Touraine wrote the most famous discussion of it in *Le Mouvement de Mai ou le Communisme Utopique* (Paris: Seuil, 1968). The analysis presented here is independent of Touraine's.

5. Clark Kerr, *The Uses of the University* (Cambridge, Mass.: Harvard, 1963).

petent. And just as the perception of domination could be universalized along the lines laid out in technocratic ideology, so could the demand for more freedom and initiative. Carrying the analogy between the university and society one step further, students discovered the general arbitrariness of the established structures of power in the society at large. This helps to explain why students sought not so much the destruction of the hierarchy of learning in the university as its destruction in the larger society they had soon to enter. Dissatisfaction with the university was displaced from the learning process and its administration along the pathways set up by technocratic ideology toward the government and the economic system.

The students confronted the tasks to which they were destined, both as teachers and executives, and rejected them. The struggle, a leaflet asserts,

> is motivated in particular by the fact that the University has become a more and more essential terrain: the intensification of the repressive reality of the University, its increasing role in the process of social reproduction, its active participation in holding together the established order (cf. the social sciences in particular), the role of science and research in economic development, all require the institution of a right to permanent contestation of the University, of its goals, its ideology, the content of its "products."

Or again:

> Today the students are becoming conscious of what is being made of them: the executives of the existing economic system, paid to make it function better. Their struggle concerns all workers because it is their struggle too: they [the students] refuse to become professors serving a teaching system which selects the sons of the bourgeoisie and eliminates the others; sociologists designing slogans for the government's electoral campaigns, psychologists charged with organizing "work teams" in the interests of the boss; executives applying a system to the workers which subjugates them as well.

Is there not an implicit anti-intellectualism in all this? The charge has often been made. Yet it would be more accurate to say that the revolt within the university was a struggle against the use of arguments from technical necessity and intellectual authority to justify a system of domination. Thus it was not intellect the students rejected, but technocracy when they wrote that they did "not want to be ruled passively any longer by 'scientific laws,' by the laws of the economy or by technical 'imperatives'."

"The Amnesty of Blinded Eyes" continues:

> Let's categorically refuse the ideology of PROFIT AND PROGRESS or other pseudo-forces of the same type. *Progress will be what we want it to be.* Let's refuse the trap of luxury and necessity—the stereotyped needs imposed separately on all, to make each worker labor in the name of the "natural laws" of the economy.

> WORKERS of every kind, let's not be duped. Do not confuse the TECHNICAL division of labor and the HIERARCHY of authority and power. The first is necessary, the second is superfluous and should be replaced by an equal exchange of our work and services within a liberated society.

In sum, the students found themselves at the leading edge of a contradiction that cuts across all modern societies, the contradiction between the enormous knowledge and wealth of these societies and the creativity they demand of their members, and the mediocre use to which this knowledge, wealth, and creativity is put.

The Texts

"The Amnesty of Blinded Eyes." This is probably the most famous document of the May Events. It was written shortly after the occupation of the Sorbonne on May 13 by a student committee that called itself "Nous Sommes en Marche" ("We are on the Way.") At first it was posted on the walls of the university, and later distributed as a leaflet and in a pamphlet with other leaflets written by the group. It has been quoted from and many of its themes analyzed in every book on the May Events. The interest of the text lies in its critique of progress and its innovative concept of cultural revolution.

"Address to All Workers." This text by the Situationist International expresses the utopian vision of the students in pungent anti-Stalinist rhetoric.[6] The Situationists linked the movement's emphasis on

---

6. For more on the role of the Situationists in the May Events, see Greil Marcus, *Lipstick Traces* (Cambridge, Mass: Harvard, 1989).

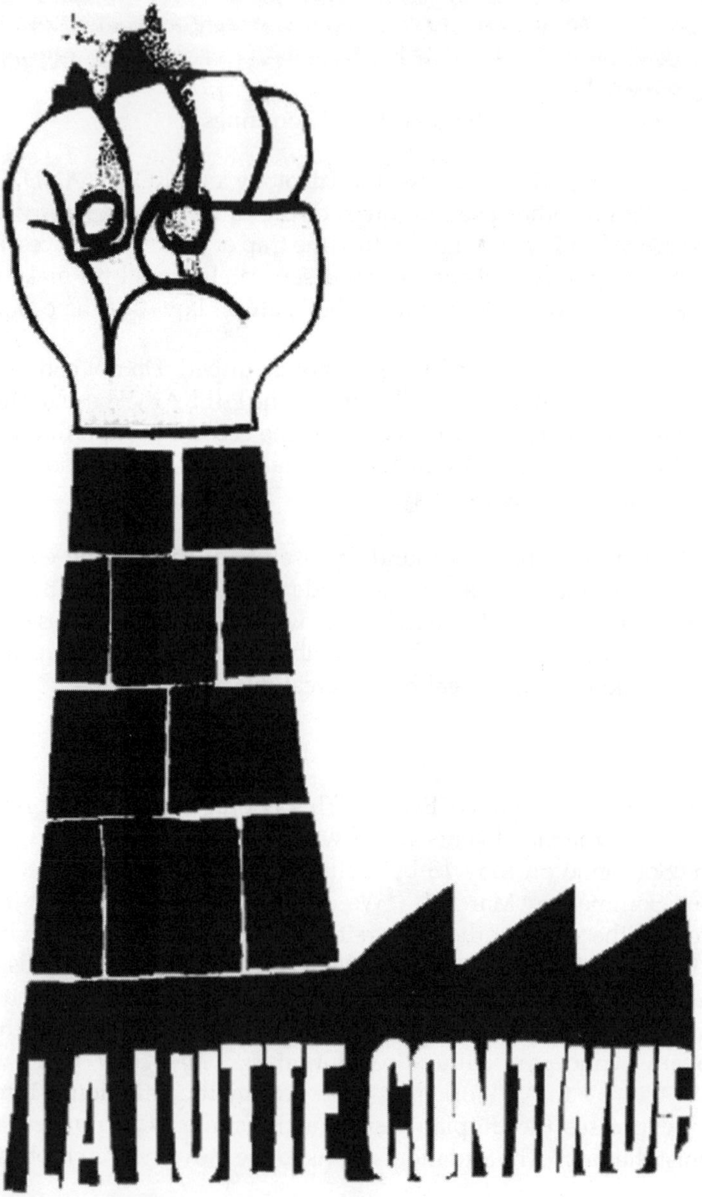
LA LUTTE CONTINUE

autonomy and self-management with the tradition of council communism—that is, a communism of workers' control and direct democracy that can be traced back to Marx's account of the Commune of Paris in 1871.

"Join the Revolutionary Commune of the Imagination." The utopianism of certain of the students was unrestrained by the spirit of seriousness. This text calls for a kind of cultural revolution that probably would not have been welcome in Mao's China.

THE AMNESTY OF BLINDED EYES

"We Are on the Way"
—Censier 453
STUDENTS-WORKERS

We demonstrated by the thousands for more than a week, and when it was necessary we fought with determination.

We believed then that our situation could change.

Today the working masses have taken advantage of our exemplary movement to ask for satisfaction of old corporative and wage demands.

These are necessary but not sufficient.

Too much or not enough.

Too much, because they cannot be obtained in the present state of the system which they implicitly challenge. Not enough, because they are addressed to a government which they have in fact abolished, but which is still being asked to make "reforms."

And this is what we are supposed to accept today!

Hundreds of wounded and injured to end up worse off than when we started.

WE DO NOT ACCEPT THIS. WE WANT THE HOPES born during these days of demonstrations to find their expression in an irreversible movement. Our ideological choice is clear: barricades are necessary, but not sufficient. Leaflets cannot replace political thought and slogans cannot replace achievements.

The following text is offered as the basis of a program. It is offered as a basis for thought and action.

It is not a doctrine, nor even a manifesto.

But it must become one.

CALL TO THE POPULATION

STUDENTS-WORKERS

We must not be duped again. We must learn to understand what we have all done in confusion and haste in the streets.

Students, we must be clearsighted and not permit ourselves to be co-opted, assimilated or "understood," with our trivial problems of "minors," of "haves," of *guilt-ridden non-proletarians.* Let's explain clearly what we want, and take the time to figure it out.

THESIS I: THERE IS NO STUDENT PROBLEM. THE STUDENT IS AN OUTDATED IDEA.

We are privileged, not with money, but with the time and the physical and material possibility of becoming aware of our situation and that of our society. We are non-proletarians; but above all, we are passive and unproductive consumers of "goods" and "culture."

TO BE A PROLETARIAN IS NEITHER A "VALUE" NOR A "FUTURE."

The proletariat must become *real workers,* with all the rights this entails. Students must cease to be cultural "haves" and future exploiters. What society has given them as individual privilege, they must immediately give back in the form of leadership.

THESIS 2: Students, let's not be cut off from the professors and the other "classes" of our society. Let's not be confined in a student pseudo-class, with its problems of economic and social integration.

THESIS 3: In the past, we were just a small minority, necessarily capable of being integrated. Today, we are a minority that is too large to be integrated, but we still have the same status as before. That is the contradiction in which we find ourselves as children of the bourgeoisie.

WE ARE NO LONGER ASSURED OF OUR FUTURE ROLE AS EXPLOITERS.

This is the origin of our revolutionary force. We must not let it slip away. *LET'S ABOLISH OURSELVES:* let's become workers so that all workers can be privileged with the right to CHOOSE THEIR OWN DESTINY.

THESIS 4: Henceforth we are workers like the others. We are an immediate and future "capital" for society and no longer merely the promise of renewal for the ruling class.

THESIS 5: STUDENTS, STOP BEING "TEMPORARY" PARASITES, *FUTURE EXPLOITERS* AND PRIVILEGED CONSUMERS. FROM NOW ON LET'S BE TRUE PRODUCERS of "goods," services, "knowledge."

THESIS 6: The full-time student is dead, the night school student as well. Everyone will study if everyone produces, consumes and studies at the same time.

THESIS 7: STUDENTS-WORKERS, we reject "consumer" society; we are wrong. Everyone should produce and consume, so that everyone can consume the equivalent of what he produces. PRODUCTION AND CONSUMPTION *can no longer be separated and abstracted from each other by the Distribution system or the technical Division of Labor.*

ACCEPT THIS BANALITY: the workers as a whole cannot consume anything which the workers as a whole do not produce. The workers as a whole must choose what they want to consume if they are to know what they must produce.

THESIS 8: Modern capitalism has aimed at the *embourgeoisement* of the working class, masked and proven by the false demands attributed to it. It was thus able to divide the world into two parts: the HAVES and all those capable of becoming such—CONFRONTED with the "temporarily" excluded of this world: the so-called Third World.

THESIS 9: THE STUDENT has become the "proletarian" of the BOURGEOISIE, and THE WORKER the "bourgeois" of the underdeveloped world.

THESIS 10: Students, workers, "haves" of all kinds, let's continue the struggle for radical change in all the societies of exploitation, oppression and mystification.

LET'S BE WHAT WE ARE AND WANT TO BECOME AND NOT WHAT THEY MAKE OF US IN SPITE OF OURSELVES.

THESIS 11: Let's reject apoliticism and revolutionism as basically identical. A few budget or wage increases will change nothing in our condition of passive objects confronted with the political, economic and technical powers.

THESIS 12: REVOLUTION IS NEITHER A LUXURY NOR AN ART: IT IS A NECESSITY WHEN EVERY OTHER MEANS HAS FAILED. Students, workers, only you can do it. Nobody will do it for you because nobody can.

THESIS 13: If our situation leads us to violence, it is because the whole society does us violence.

REFUSE THE VIOLENCE of "happiness" that is imposed on everyone—the scandalous happiness of overwork, of the sale of our labor and our vital energy in exchange for a bauble in black and white or color, which will then be used the better to enslave us and deprive us of our humanity.

THESIS 14: Students-workers, from now on we refuse this infernal cycle and this slow death. We *demand and will obtain* the right of all workers at all levels of responsibility of consumption-production and production-consumption to decide together in solidarity—in the exchange of their services—what they want their working humanity to be.

TO WORK is TO REALIZE ONE'S LIFE through a NECESSARY AND FREE activity. THE DIVISION OF LABOR is the EXCHANGE of services and HUMAN SOLIDARITY through mastered techniques.

THESIS 15: Students-workers, let's accept the means to our ends. If we want a radical change in our condition, we will not get it by dialogue, because dialogue was broken off long ago. If we want a mere reorganization of our "privileges" or a few more baubles, let's not delude ourselves with revolution because it will cost us dearly.

STUDENTS-WORKERS LET'S CHOOSE!

BUT CHOOSE QUICKLY!

THESIS 16: Let's be something other than the "characters in a tragi-comedy" which is no longer even funny. LET'S BE TRUE ACTORS!

THESIS 17: To act is not to demand the impossible in the present system, but to change things so that we no longer have to demand a "role" and rights—it is to render charity and "good works" the gift of their sacrifices.

THESIS 18: Let's reject the dialogue of the deaf composed of words, but reject also that of brutal and conventional force. NEITHER TAKE REFUGE BEHIND OUR DEMANDS NOR BEHIND OUR BARRICADES. LET'S ATTACK!

THESIS 19: Let's accept our responsibilities toward ourselves and others. We must categorically refuse the ideology of PROFIT AND PROGRESS or other pseudo-forces of the same type. *Progress will be what we want it to be.* Let's reject the entanglement of luxury and necessity—stereotyped needs imposed separately on all, so that each worker labors in the name of the "natural laws" of the economy.

THESIS 20: WORKER, decide with all the workers, *competent or not,* on your output, your "marketing."

THESIS 21: Let's reject all the divisions perpetuated consciously or by necessity between Proletarian and Bourgeois. *Proletarian abolish yourself.* Become a true worker and there will no longer be bourgeois but only workers. We must also reject the intellectual autonomy of the technocrats. Once work was separated from the person who performed it, once this living contradiction, the "CONSUMER PRODUCT" was forged, it was necessary to valorize the only thing which remained: raw WORK, FORCE, VIOLENCE.

This made possible the separation of engineers from workers, creators from "operators," humanists from scientists, the "useful" from the "parasites," to create a hierarchy of "VALUES" so that each becomes a cop for the other, the better to rule the workers in the most complete "Freedom."

THESIS 22: WORKERS of every kind, don't let's be duped. Do not confuse the TECHNICAL division of labor and the HIERARCHY of authority and power. The first is necessary, the second is superfluous and should be replaced by an equal exchange of our work and services within a liberated society.

THESIS 23: Let's also reject the division of *science* and *ideology*, the most pernicious division of all because we secrete it ourselves. We do not want to be passively governed anymore by "scientific laws," by the laws of the economy or by technical "imperatives."

Science is an "art," the originality of which is to have possible applications outside of itself. However, it is only normative for itself. We must reject its mystifying imperialism, which excuses every abuse and regression, even within science itself. Let's replace it with a real choice among the possibilities it offers.

THESIS 24: LET'S ALSO REJECT the clichés of revolutionary language, which confuses the issues to avoid posing the real problems. Let's always ask *which* revolution is at issue.

THESIS 25: Don't answer when asked "where we are going." We are not in power, we do not have to be "positive," to justify our "excesses."

But if we do reply, that too must mean that we *will* the means of our ends, that is to say, if not state power, at least *a power excluding every form of oppression and violence as the basis of its existence and the means of its survival.*

THESIS 26: Let's not allow our goals to be co-opted any longer by all the tired revolutionaries and the existing institutions. *WE WANT AND WILL GET production AND consumption to control each other and BOTH CONTROLLED BY ALL OF US, WORKERS OF THE WHOLE WORLD UNITED IN THE SAME NECESSITY OF LIVING, AND ACTING SO THAT THIS NECESSITY IS NO LONGER ALIENATING.*

THESIS 27: Like the bourgeoisie in its day, the proletariat was revolutionary, that is to say that it could not engage in dialogue without radically transforming society. Some tried and are still trying to strip it of this power by dividing the workers and by constituting a false "peaceful co-existence" between the bourgeoisie and the proletariat in the face of the STARVING OF THE EARTH. This "harmony of interests" is based on RACISM, and on the various intellectual and financial hierarchies associated with work. The whole is justified by reified fragments of an ideology from the last century.

THESIS 28: Students, if you are considered to be *privileged,* it is the better to integrate you into this industrial-bureau-technocracy of profit and progress by deluding you with economic-scientific imperatives. The significance of this designation is clear. For the workers, such privileged people can only be *petty bourgeois provocateurs.* For the ruling class, they are *ingrates and "romantic" hysterics.* The starting point is different, the mystification is the same and has the same goal: defensive reductionism.

THESIS 29: The bourgeois revolution was juridical—the proletarian revolution was "economic." *Ours will be social and cultural,* so that man may become himself and no longer be satisfied with a "humanistic" ideology.

THESIS 30: Finally, let's reject the ideologies of the "total man," which offer us a "final goal"—the end of history—and this in the name of "progress," *the better to reject progression.*

WORKERS-STUDENTS, we are the revolutionary "class," the bearers of the *dominant ideology,* because our aim is to abolish ourselves as a class along with all other classes.

ALL WE WANT IS TO BE YOUNG WORKERS

And this we propose to thousands of young workers, young or old, intellectual or manual, so that they may be like us and we like them.

ONCE AGAIN, *we must abolish every privilege,* all the hidden barriers and for that we will have to struggle with all our might and by every means—until victory, which can only be *provisionally final.*

REREAD THIS CALL AGAIN AND AGAIN

BECOME ITS AUTHOR—Correct it—recopy it

DISTRIBUTE IT IN MILLIONS OF COPIES

POST IT

AND *WHEN WE ARE ALL ITS AUTHORS, the old world will crumble to make way for*

THE UNION OF THE WORKERS OF ALL NATIONS.

"We are on the way"

ADDRESS TO ALL WORKERS

Comrades,

What we have already done in France haunts Europe and will soon threaten all the ruling classes in the world, from bureaucrats in Moscow and Peking to billionaires in Washington and Tokyo. Just as *we have made Paris dance,* so the international proletariat will storm the capitals of all the nations, all the citadels of alienation. Occupation of factories and public buildings throughout the country has not only blocked the functioning of the economy, but above all, has challenged the society as a whole. A profound movement leads almost all sectors of the population to desire to change life. From now on this is a revolutionary movement, which lacks only *the consciousness of what it has already done* to really possess this revolution.

What forces will try to save capitalism? The regime must fall if it does not maintain itself by threatening a recourse to arms (accompanied by a hypothetical call for elections which could only take place after the capitulation of the movement), or even immediate armed repression. As for an eventual government of the left, it too will try to defend the old world by concessions and by force. The best [element or guardian?] of this "popular government" would be the so-called Communist Party, the party of the Stalinist bureaucrats, which only began to envisage the fall of Gaullism from the moment when it saw it could no longer serve as its main protection. Such a transitional government would really be a "Kerenskyism" only if the Stalinists were defeated.[7] This will essentially depend on the workers' consciousness and capacity for autonomous organization: those who have already rejected the insignificant agreements that so delighted the union leaders must discover that they cannot "get" much more in the framework of the existing economy, but that they can *take everything* by transforming the whole basis for their own benefit. The bosses can hardly pay more, but they can disappear.

The present movement has not been politicized by going beyond the miserable union demands for wages and pensions, falsely presented as "social problems." It is already beyond *politics:* it *poses the social problem* in its simple truth. The revolution, in preparation for more

---

7. Some revolutionaries hoped that, just as Kerensky's liberal government in Russia had fallen to the Bolsheviks, so a coalition government of Socialists and Communists would fall to the revolutionary movement in France in 1968.

than a century, has returned. It can assert itself only in its own forms. It is already too late for bureaucratic-revolutionary patchwork. When a recently de-Stalinized André Barjonet calls for the formation of a common organization that would bring together "all the authentic forces of the revolution . . . whether they follow Trotsky, Mao, anarchism, situationism," we can only recall that those who today follow Trotsky or Mao, not to speak of the pathetic "Anarchist Federation," have nothing to do with the present revolution.[8] The bureaucrats can change their minds now about what they will call "authentically revolutionary"; the authentic revolution need not change its condemnation of bureaucracy.

At the present moment, given the power the workers hold, and what we know about the parties and unions, the only path open to the workers is the direct seizure of the economy and all aspects of the reconstruction of social life by unitary rank and file committees. In this way, they can assert their autonomy in relation to all political or union leadership, maintain their own self-defense, and federate themselves at the regional and national levels. By following this path they will become the only real power in the country, the power of the workers' councils. Failing this, the proletariat will again become a passive object, because it is "revolutionary or it is nothing." It will go back to its television sets.

What defines the power of the councils? The dissolution of all external power; direct and total democracy; practical unification of decision-making and implementation; delegates who can be recalled at any time by their electors; the abolition of hierarchy and independent specializations; conscious management and transformation of all the conditions of liberated life; permanent creative participation of the masses; internationalist extension and coordination. The demands of the present are no less. Self-management is nothing less than this. *Beware of* modernist *co-opters* of every kind (even including priests) who begin by talking about self-management, or even workers' councils, without granting this *minimum,* because in fact they want to save their bureaucratic functions, the privileges of their intellectual specialization, or their future as petty bosses!

What is necessary today has been necessary since the beginning of the proletarian revolutionary project. At stake has always been the autonomy of the working class. We were struggling for the abolition of the wage system, commodity production, the State. The goal was to

---

8. Recall that Barjonet was a high official in the CGT who left the union and called for the creation of a revolutionary organization at the Charléty meeting.

make history conscious, abolishing all separations and "everything that exists independently from the individuals." The proletarian revolution has spontaneously outlined its adequate forms in the councils, in St. Petersburg in 1905, as well as in Turin in 1920, in Catalonia in 1936, in Budapest in 1956. Each time, the survival of the old society or the formation of new exploiting classes has required the suppression of the councils. The working class now knows its enemies, and the methods of action that are its own. "The revolutionary organization had to learn that it can no longer *fight alienation in alienated forms*" (*Society of the Spectacle*).[9] The workers' councils are clearly the only solution, because all the other forms of revolutionary struggle have led to the contrary of what they wanted.

w/ such a broad statement essential to define what workers' councils are and look like (only vague if don't have historical understanding) also propoganda/leaflet not theoretical text

JOIN THE REVOLUTIONARY COMMUNE OF THE IMAGINATION

The Cultural Revolution cannot be reconciled with the economic and juridical structures of bourgeois society because it is one of the many aspects of the *revolutionary* movement.

This principle has been clearly demonstrated by the so-called avant-garde theaters, which have in fact been at the avant-garde of the return to work on June 9, 1968. In answer to the appeals of the Revolutionary Committee for Cultural Agitation (CRAC), revolutionary students and artists therefore interrupted shows in the name of solidarity with the strikers at Flins and the Radio-Television, and publically denounced the use which the mercantile system makes of Art, whether avant-garde or not, and ideology, whether it be left or elsewhere.

---

9. *Society of the Spectacle* was the chief theoretical work of the "Situationist International," a small group of young radicals with a large influence on the ideas and language of the May Events. See Guy Debord, *La Société du Spectacle* (Paris: Gallimard, 1995).

The government is now busy neutralizing the workers' movement of contestation and the revolutionary germs which it carries in its heart.

The ideologues, the official artists, and the whole capitalist system of production and distribution of art and theater—including the system's established union organizations—contribute to the operation by sabotaging the workers' strike, and by inviting the public to return to the fallacious universe of the commercialized dream.

Students-Artists-Workers: open a breach in the cultural system of the bourgeoisie.

Let's decree the Revolutionary Commune of the Imagination. The Latin Quarter is a ghetto of the most underhanded sort, where culture is confined for the benefit of a few and commercialized in limited editions. It is the ghetto of intellectual complacency, in which the sheep proudly claim the brand they wear on their ass.

Break these degrading chains.

Occupy all the territories reserved for the private paradises of cultural alienation.

Purge the region of those closed places where products conditioned or tolerated by the cultural system (theater, cinema, galleries) are sold pell-mell to the privileged few.

Open wide the streets, the universities, the high schools, to creation and invention.

Welcome all the excluded, the poor and the oppressed of bourgeois culture, on the ruins of its Pantheons.

Transform our ghetto into a fortress of liberty and imagination.

Liberate, together with all the workers, all the creative forces repressed by our society.

Comrades, the Revolution is a daily event.

It is a joyous celebration, an explosion which liberates the energies.

Let's get organized.

Let's invent our means of action.

Let's unite our energies:

For the free exercise of imagination in the streets.

For the transformation of the Sorbonne into an international revolutionary center for cultural agitation open to all the workers and self-managed by the participants, who would have the following minimum program:

—impose, coordinate and support the subversion and the destruction of the bourgeois cultural order everywhere cultural guerilla actions arise like those that have begun to break out in industrialized capitalist societies.

—impose and materialize in new forms of civilization the creative and revolutionary forces transmitted by the workers of the cities and the countryside, stifled and frustrated by the bourgeois cultural system.

—realize practically as well as theoretically, the establishment of partial self-management to prepare for the generalized self-management of society.

For the occupation of all the theaters in the Latin Quarter and their utilization as operational bases for the transformation of the exterior space into a vast stage of the possible, where everyone becomes the actor and the author of the collective socio-dramatic happening.

For the occupation of all the movie houses, galleries and dance halls and their transformation into operational bases for the appropriation of the entire urban space (walls, sidewalks, roads, rivers and sky) as a framework for image, sound and plastic expression in a gigantic sketch of permanent invention at the service of all.

For a Practice of Imagination in the Service of the Revolution.

Unite, pass to theoretical and practical action in the C.R.I. (Research and Intervention Commandos)

Enlist at the CRAC.
Free Sorbonne-Odeon

Essay II. In the Service of the People

"Obedience begins with conscience and conscience with disobedience."[10]

The struggles of May briefly dislocated one of the structural bases of capitalist democracy: the allegiance of the middle strata to the established parties and institutions. Opposition exploded among teachers, journalists, other employees in the "culture industry," social service workers, civil servants, and even among some middle and lower level business executives. So much for the image of a politically passive and socially conformist middle class, put forward in the classic analyses of "white-collar" labor of C. Wright Mills and William Whyte. The students found their own revolt embedded in the much broader movements of the occupational groups to which the university licenses the entry.

The May Events produced a flowering of theories to explain this phenomenon.[11] This is not the place to review these discussions. The

---

10. Graffiti from the walls of Paris during the May Events. "Grève au Ministère des Finances: On Debré-Ye." "Grève Sur Place au Ministère de l'Equipement (20 Mai–8 Juin)," Cahiers de Mai, no. 2, July 1968. "Toute une Ville Découvre le Pouvoir Populaire," Cahiers de Mai, no. 1, May 15, 1968, p. 6. "Manifesto," a leaflet that exists in several versions with different authors is apparently due to the Comité de Coordination des Cadres Contestataires. It is translated in Schnapp and Vidal-Naquet, *The French Student Uprising* (Boston: Beacon, 1971), pp. 566–567. "Les Bureaux de Recherches," Action, June 24, 1968.

11. For new working-class interpretations, see Touraine, op. cit., or A. Glucksmann,

study of the role of the employed middle strata in the May Events cannot resolve the theoretical problems, but it can teach us how these strata understood themselves and acted in support of a developing revolutionary movement. During the May Events there were brave attempts to convince them that they were ordinary workers. Roger Garaudy, among others, argued that engineers, technicians, office employees, and executives were "proletarianized," "because the mechanization of administrative tasks and managerial functions increasingly eliminates the frontier between the employee as a manipulator of computers, to give an example, and the laborer working under conditions of automation."[12]

In practice, however, the middle strata in revolt did not see themselves as just another sector of the working class and, in contrast with the latter, their demands were primarily social and political. Their protest focused on the absurdity of "consumer society"; they denounced the bureaucratic and hierarchical organization of their work and demanded the right to participate in the determination of its goals. The most advanced struggles of the middle strata were distinguished in another way from workers' struggles. The workers' movement spoke in the name of the "people"; the middle strata expressed their desire to switch their allegiance from the state and the capitalist system to the "people." This language tended to imply that they were indeed in the middle of the social hierarchy, neither rulers nor ruled. This intermediary position reflects the ambiguous role of "knowledge workers" in a technocratic society, caught between traditional elites and the mass of the population which is now administered in new technocratic forms. Some examples may make this clear.

1. Education. During the May Events high schools and universities in solidarity with the movement declared their "autonomy." As one leaflet explained it, "The autonomy of public education is an act of political secession from a government which has definitively failed in

---

Stratégie et Révolution en France 1968 (Paris: Christian Bourgois, 1968). For a defense of the traditional view of the middle strata as part of the petty bourgeoisie, see the Maoist response to Glucksmann, *Les Etudiants, les Cadres et la Révolution,* published by the Centre Universitaire d'Etude et de Formation Marxiste-Léniniste, 1968. The Communist Party was divided by this debate, with the traditional option predominating during the period of the Events. Cf. Claude Prévost, "Les Foundations de l'Idéologie Gauchiste," La Nouvelle Critique, June 1968. Roger Garaudy presented an alternative view, based on the notion of proletarianization of the middle strata, in "La Révolte et la Révolution," La Démocratie Nouvelle, April–May 1968.

12. Garaudy, op. cit., 9.

its task of defending the real interests of the community in the educational sphere." But what did "autonomy" mean? Did the university in revolt hope to isolate itself from society? In a lengthy leaflet a group of leftist faculty explained why it could not do so:

> The principal victims of the present operation and organization of the educational system are, by definition, outside the system because they have been eliminated from it; consequently, the groups whose voices have not been heard in university discussions, discussions between beneficiaries of the system, are the very ones who would have the most direct interest in a real transformation of the system. . . .
>
> Every attempt to call academic institutions into question which does not bear fundamentally on the function they serve in eliminating the lower classes, and consequently, on the socially conservative function of the school system, is necessarily illusory. . . .
>
> In declaring the University 'open to the workers,' even if it is only a question here of a symbolic and illusory gesture, the students have at least shown that they were aware of a problem which cannot be resolved except by acting on the mechanisms which forbid certain classes access to higher education.[13]

It was out of reflection on problems such as these that the students concretized their demand for "autonomy" with proposals for "permanent education for all" and invitations to workers to participate in the reform of the university. Autonomy was thus not an end in itself; it was precisely through autonomy that the university attempted to switch its class allegiance.

2. Communication. The communications industry was also thrown into turmoil during May. The nationalized sector was struck by employees demanding "a radio and television in the service of all and not of a party." This was the counterpart of student-faculty demands for a democratization of education. Like the students, the personnel of the radio-television company sought liberation from the stifling supervi-

---

13. Among the signatories were a number of prominent scholars, including P. Bourdieu, R. Castel, J. Cuisenier, A. Culioli, J. Derrida, L. Goldmann, J. Le Goff, E. Leroy-Ladurie, L. Marin, J. B. Pontalis, and P. Ricoeur. This text is reprinted in the French edition of Schnapp and Vidal-Naquet, *La Commune Etudiante* (Paris: Seuil, 1968), p. 695ff.

sion of the Gaullist state through increased autonomy. In particular, they demanded the right to tell the truth. In the context of the May Events, that demand was fairly clear. It meant supporting the movement by mirroring its own activities back to it.

3. Civil Service. During May, government employees closed many of their own ministries in solidarity with the movement. The pattern of protest was similar in every case: a combination of demands for more democratic working conditions and an end to policies the civil servants judged opposed to the interests of the people. Civil servants, like students and communications workers, attempted to include the previously excluded, and to switch their allegiances from the state to the population, as though they themselves represented a middle term.

Even the usually staid Ministry of Finances was involved. Civil servants there simply reenacted the model of the student movement, complete with occupations, general assemblies, and reform commissions. A descriptive leaflet tells the story:

> While the students rose in all the universities of France and ten million strikers united against the iniquities of the economic system, the prodigious popular movement of May 68 touched the civil servants of the principal ministries, where traditional administrative structures have been profoundly shaken.
>
> The personnel assembly of the central administration of economy and finances, meeting the 21st of May, decided *to continue the strike.* At the Ministry of Finances, as in the majority of associated services and at the National Institute of Statistics, the civil servants stopped work and occupied their offices.
>
> May 21, a demonstration in the Rue de Rivoli drew 500 civil servants from Finances demanding an administration in the service of the people and a "radical change of economic and social policy."

Similar events occurred in the Ministry of Urban Affairs and Housing, which issued a leaflet containing the following significant paragraph.

> Civil servants in the service of the community, we have become, paradoxically, and for many of us against our will, the symbol of red tape. As a result of an erroneous conception of the role of the Administration and the lack of consultation in decision-making and implementation, instead of being the driving force of

L'INTOX VIENT A DOMICILE

Urban Affairs and Housing, we are the brakes that everyone would like to see disappear.

In cases like these the professionalist ideology of "public service" glides imperceptibly into the Maoist rhetoric of "service to the people."

4. Business Executives. No doubt most business executives were hostile to the movement; however, a significant minority supported it. As one commentator noted:

> [I]n the Loire-Atlantique impressive numbers of executives were in solidarity with the workers, something never seen before. But support for wage demands was not the main point; the theme of management cemented the union. The executives were frustrated by the excessive centralization of public enterprises; they remain in their offices, signing papers, but they have no decision-making power.

On May 20, fifteen hundred executives met at the Sorbonne and declared their sympathy with the movement. Several hundred seized the Paris headquarters of the union of executives and engineers and called for a general strike. In a leaflet issued on May 24, they demanded "The elaboration of concrete solutions for the democratization of management and of the general economic decision making process. The goal of fulfillment of the personality, in work as well as in leisure, must be substituted for the usual goals of profitability and expansion."

5. Technical Experts. The Events even reached a think tank working for the government. The researchers there earned good livings making surveys and studies for government ministries, usually concerning public works projects. Yet even before May they suffered from a distinct malaise. They were aware that their work, on becoming the "property" of the purchasing ministry, served to justify preestablished policies or was ignored where it conflicted with them. Often the researchers felt these policies were not in the best interests of the very populations they were asked to study. This is an alienating situation and during May, "It suddenly seemed intolerable that the researcher have in the final analysis no control over the product of his work."

Yet there could be no question of claiming control for the sake of personal satisfaction. No sooner had the researchers gone on strike than they attempted to join up with the people whose interests they wished to serve. Their union declared, "The workers of the National Union of

Social Sciences affirm their will to see their work placed in the service of the workers and not in the service of management and the capitalist state apparatus." Concretely, they provided financial aid to poorer strikers and, in one case, made a free study of employment in the Paris suburbs at the request of the local unions.

These examples illustrate a common pattern. In May 1968 the French middle strata did not so much feel useless or guilty about their privileges as misused by those in command of the society. Their radical stand is best understood as an appeal to the population to redirect their work into more humane and productive channels. In 1971, when the French Communist Party revised its attitude toward the middle strata, its theoreticians described their new political potentialities.

> Before these transformations emerged, the support for working-class struggles by the middle strata and especially by intellectuals appeared as a rallying to the proletarian cause. Today there is no longer any question of individuals rallying to the cause, but of an entente to be established between social strata having common interests that can build a democratic future together.[14]

This statement of the case reflects the experience of the May Events and helps to explain the subsequent rise of the electoral alliance of the Communist Party, primarily representing workers, and the Socialist Party which, after the Events, came to represent a large fraction of the middle strata.

The Texts

"The In-House Strike at the Ministry of Urban Affairs."   The author of this article, a civil servant at the ministry, describes the political struggle in a government bureaucracy. The text is translated from the *Les Cahiers de Mai*, no. 2, July, 1968.

"Research Bureaus: Wall-to-Wall Carpeting and Revolution." In this article, a student observer describes the strike in a government-supported think tank. The article was published in *Action*, June 24, 1968.

"Journal of a Neighborhood Action Committee."   During May and June, "action committees" sprang up everywhere, mobilizing the energies of local groups in schools, neighborhoods, and workplaces.

---

14. *Le Capitalisme Monopoliste d'Etat* (Paris: Editions Sociales, 1971), vol. I, p. 240.

This article describes the activities of such a committee in a middle-class neighborhood of Paris. The article first appeared in *Les Cahiers de Mai,* no. 3, August–September, 1968.

THE "IN-HOUSE" STRIKE AT THE MINISTRY OF URBAN AFFAIRS

(May 20–June 8)

The active "in-house and unlimited" strike that took place from May 20 to June 8 at the Ministry of Urban Affairs testifies to the breadth of revolutionary ferment in French society.

The very day before, on May 19, anyone who had spoken of such an extraordinary possibility would have been considered a bit mad. In any case, the leaders of the General Union of the Federation of Civil Servants (CGT) did not foresee anything like it. It is doubtful that they expected any significant action at all to take place in the civil service. On Sunday, May 19, when the strike movement had been spreading rapidly for a week already, activists who showed up to hear the news at Federation headquarters, Rue de Solferino, were surprised to find the offices empty; they had expected to find the union leadership meeting and deliberating on what to do. At the end of a corridor, they finally discovered a comrade on duty who informed them that the Federation had prepared a leaflet inviting civil servants to decide for themselves the nature of their future job action.

The comrades could pick up the leaflet on Monday morning. In short, rank-and-file militants would have to come and get it on their own.

And so this leaflet was distributed to the civil servants in front of the Ministry the next morning. On the other hand, what we rather improperly call the "Inter Union Council" (that is, the tacit association of the four Unions in the order of their numeric importance: the FO, CGT, CFDT and C.G.C.) had agreed to call a general assembly of the personnel for 1:30 P.M.

To the great surprise of numerous union activists, this general assembly enthusiastically endorsed:

1) an "in-house and unlimited" strike
2) the convocation every morning of the general assembly of the personnel, which was to become the directing organ of the strike and which was to elect a new president daily. The role of this latter was to be limited to guaranteeing free debate (thus eighteen presidents succeeded each other until June 8)
3) the creation of five advisory commissions that would submit their proposals to the general assembly. Their missions were:
   a) Reform of the Administration
   b) Reform of the structures of the Ministry of Urban Affairs and Housing
   c) A List of Demands
   d) A Liaison and Information Committee
   e) A Permanent Action Committee and Open Forum.

The General Assembly immediately contacted Ministry personnel working in another building on the Boulevard St. Germain which also contained the office of the Minister—at that time Mr. Ortoli. That same evening, the strike spread to the Boulevard St. Germain as a result of a decision taken by a General Assembly like our own. It also spread to three housing research centers in annexes of the Ministry.

WERE WE REPRESENTATIVE?

One aspect of the movement seemed entirely new, even unprecedented. The General Assembly decided that, even while carrying out an "in-house" strike (that is, on the premises of the Ministry), it would not prevent non-strikers from entering their offices. In addition, the General Assemblies held every morning were declared open to all personnel, strikers or non-strikers. Theoretically, the non-strikers could thus put a stop to the movement at any moment.

But they represented only 20 to 30 percent of the personnel, which comprised about fourteen hundred civil servants and temporary workers, so that the few maneuvers some of them tried were easily countered.

In fact, the General Assembly was truly representative of a clear majority of the Ministry's personnel, although an average of only 100 to 150 civil servants and staff attended each session. We were firmly convinced of this, but we had no formal proof The Minister's office also tried to get information on our "representativity." As is usual during strikes, it circulated attendance sheets in the offices. The General Assembly then appealed to the non-strikers to refuse to sign such sheets and to give them back, unsigned, to the Minister who finally gave up trying to get them signed. He resigned himself to requesting the "approximate percentage" of strikers, but even had we wanted to satisfy his request, how could we determine this percentage even within a margin of a few points?

Indeed, from the beginning of the strike, we noticed that a very large number of civil servants and staff lived outside Paris, often far away; their absence may have been explained by the absence of transportation due to the difficulty of getting gas. They were probably not militant non-strikers, but could they therefore be counted as strikers?

The answer, which provoked many frank discussions, came from the people in question themselves during the last General Assembly on June 8.

There was transportation again. Gas was available. It is worth noting that the political situation had changed quite a bit in two weeks. Nevertheless, when it came time to select a room for this last General Assembly, we hesitated. It was possible that we were isolated and the usual meeting place was big enough because our colleagues would not wish to seem to share our cause, especially at the last minute when the situation was evolving in a direction that could appear unfavorable to our movement.

In the end, we chose a large room for the General Assembly of that last morning, and it was attended by about 700 civil servants and staff. We passed the first test.

But there was more to come. The General Assembly had to debate an important and significant question. After many difficulties, the unions had accepted our plan for a delegation to negotiate with the Minister, consisting of four delegates designated by the unions and two delegates chosen by the General Assembly. But the Minister recognized only the unions' representatives and refused to receive the delegation.

The president of the General Assembly then proposed a vote on a short motion requesting the union organizations "to demand that the Minister allow the elected delegates from the General Assembly to participate in the negotiations." Of the 700 civil servants and staff members present, a vast majority not only participated in the vote but approved the adoption of this motion, which constituted an indirect approval of the main lines of our activities.

It goes without saying that once the union delegates sat down with the Minister, they did not eagerly defend this motion. For 18 days, they had looked upon this sovereign General Assembly with irritation, impatient to restore their own control.

The greatest difficulties came from the FO leaders. This is the strongest union at the Ministry of Urban Affairs and Housing. We were even fortunate enough to be visited by the federal leaders of its Union Headquarters who tried to put pressure on us with arguments that were, on the whole, rather insulting. "Your strike is illegal," they told us. "In other ministries, sanctions are already looming on the horizon, etc."

At the CGT the situation was more complex. Because there were some comrades who believed in the ideas of the movement, the union local of the Ministry participated in the activities decided upon by the General Assemblies, but for 18 days no leader of the local union, no leader of the Federation showed his face at the Ministry. They had vanished into thin air! Nevertheless, as we were to find out on May 30, they did not think about us the less on that account.

The General Assembly decided to write up a leaflet to publicize our strike and to distribute it in front of the Ministries that were not on strike to incite them to join our movement. But, since we received no information at all from the Union, nobody could say exactly which ministries were on strike and which were not. So a comrade called the Rue de Solferino and got some vague bits of information which led us to distribute our leaflets in front of the Ministry of Agriculture. There, a union activist came to meet us and said: "Thanks for your leaflet, comrades. What you're doing is very good. But you are knocking at the wrong door. We have been on strike since May 24!"

A few days later this leaflet was to infuriate comrade Furst, the Secretary of the Federation of Technical and Administrative Personnel. "You have no right to do this!" he cried at the Rue de Solferino office. "We don't want to hear any more about you! We are opposed! Is that clear?"

It must also be noted that the Communist Party cell of our ministry did not meet once during those 18 days, and only four of its approximately thirty members participated in the movement.

One of our comrades, an activist in the CFDT, told us that he had problems with his leaders that were rather similar to ours.

THE WORK OF THE COMMISSIONS

A rather considerable amount of work was accomplished during the 18 days of the "in-house" strike. Even on Saturdays, even on Ascension day and the Monday of Pentecost, the comrades came to the Ministry.

On the first floor at the Quai de Passy, we have five conference rooms with mobile partitions, where the commissions could meet comfortably. The most active was indisputably the one concerned with the reform of the Administration. Here is the preamble of the motion that was adopted by the General Assembly at its initiative on (I think) the 24th of May. For us it is a kind of charter:

MOTION

The personnel of the Ministry of Urban Affairs and Housing has stopped work in its domain, the Administration. By this act it expresses its will to participate in the strike movement for the transformation of society.

For months in some cases, for years in others, we have witnessed the decay of an administrative system incapable of solving the problems of urban development and housing, even as we have become more and more aware of the increasing needs.

We have suffered from very difficult, sometimes even humiliating working conditions, as well as from the disparities in pay which have been imposed on us.

We have been subjected to decisions in which we had no say except through powerless paritary commissions or committees.

We have worked under astonishing conditions of irresponsibility, crushed by a bureaucratic system that is both impotent and absurd.

Civil servants in the service of the community, we have become, paradoxically, and for many of us against our will, the symbol of red tape. As a result of an erroneous conception of the role of the Administration and the lack of consultation in decision-making and implementation, instead of being the driving force of Urban Affairs and Housing, we are the brakes that everyone would like to see disappear.

A very difficult material situation, irresponsibility, impotence; since Monday, May 20 we have been working to find solutions to all this—to make an inventory of the problems and to define the goals and means of a renovated Administration.

Other texts establish the first principles of this reform of the Administration while describing some of its old and new vices with the sobriety of a clinical examination. Space is obviously lacking here to publish these documents, which would no doubt be read with interest and also with a feeling of relief, not only by numerous civil servants but by the citizens themselves. In the near future, perhaps, the *Cahiers de Mai* should put together the various contributions on this same subject written during May, from one end of the country to the other, and publish special numbers in order to compare our experiences with those of all the others who, we now learn with much delay, were involved in activities comparable to ours.

WHAT IS LEFT?

That is a question which will be difficult to answer before some time has passed.

For the moment our main demands have not been satisfied.

We wanted the principle of these General Assemblies to become a permanent reality. They constitute an embryo of real democracy which, in the eyes of many, could be further developed and could transform many things. Discussions were often quite heated but nobody left the room slamming the door.

We also wanted our commissions to become administrative commissions. But there too we were faced with a final refusal.

What remains is the fact that, during those 18 days, we glimpsed something and felt it as a new possibility. Numerous barriers have fallen, notably between civil servants and the rest of the staff. The informal mode of address (*tutoiement*) has been spreading. (This detail will bring a smile to the lips only of those who do not know the Administration.)[15] Young people who had never been active in a party or union, nor even spoken about politics during office hours, suddenly volunteered to distribute leaflets in the street. Even old time civil servants, occasionally high ranking ones, got an inkling, after fifteen or twenty years of absurdity, that a different life in a different society was perhaps in the nature of things. And finally, there was a very great solidarity vis-à-vis the students, and through this solidarity, one could say, there emerged a still diffuse but very real feeling of solidarity toward the striking workers. "Those people," it was said, "those people are like us."

---

15. The reference here is to the informal word for "you" and the corresponding verb conjugation that in France was used primarily within the family and among schoolmates and close friends until quite recently. Its use in a government ministry implies a rejection of hierarchy and an attempt to establish a comradely atmosphere.

RESEARCH BUREAUS: WALL-TO-WALL
CARPETING AND REVOLUTION

La Defense. The Bellini neighborhood. Lawn. Fountains. Discreet bushes. An entrance hall the luxury of which is somewhat forced. An elevator with a call phone. Fourth floor. Offices.

This is a Research Bureau. The business has about 80 employees, perhaps 60 of whom are executives. The latter earn between 2000 and 4000 Francs[16]; moreover, there are substantial fringe benefits: a cafeteria which is nothing like a student cafeteria or even a company canteen. The prices: two or three Francs, according to income. It is two-thirds subsidized. The employees are paid for a thirteenth month; there is a co-op. There are expense accounts for the rather numerous trips outside Paris (which effectively doubles the wages), and a 42.5 hour work week; and, of course, if you ever feel like leaving at four in the afternoon, or not coming in at all, no one will bother you.

Under these conditions, why on earth should the employees have gone on strike during the Events?

AN EXEMPLARY STRIKE

The employees went on strike the very first day out of solidarity with the students who were nursing their first wounds, and with the workers who, from hour to hour, were beginning unlimited work stoppages. Out of solidarity alone? Yes and no. In the beginning no doubt this kind of motive was decisive for most of them. In a more obscure way it was perhaps also the desire to be associated with an anti-Gaullist movement, just to join "the left."

There would certainly be a lot to say about the population of these research bureaus: what is the political background of the research consultants and investigators? We will come back to this later. Clearer demands soon appeared: concerning the company at first, relating to problems of internal organization that were really rather minor. But above all, as was clearly stated at the first meeting, the slogan of the movement was: "No" to today's research bureaus!

To give an example: an administrator in a ministry (usually Urban Development, Social and Economic Affairs, Housing, or Transportation)

---

16. A 1968 franc was roughly equivalent to $1 today.

needs to know what the population affected by his decision will think of it in order to validate one of his working hypotheses. He entrusts the implementation of this study to this or that team from this or that research bureau, and signs a contract.

In the case of the C.E.R.A.U. (Study and Research Center for Urban Development) with which we are concerned here, around 90 percent of their contracts are with ministries. Other possible "clients," such as municipalities, obviously lack the means to enter into such contracts which can easily involve millions.

But the ministerial client is not the only source of income. The company needs a permanent financial base, a bank or similar institution to take care of its investments, such as expansion of the premises, acquisition of electronic material, funds to cover over-runs. In this case it is the *Caisse des Dépots et Consignations* of which Bloch-Lainé is the best known director. Consequently, the money from ministerial contracts simply fulfills the role of subsidizing operating costs.

The two initial political givens are clear: on the one hand the company can be held accountable. That is, if it strikes it takes a risk with its *clients* (the ministries). In as far as the laws of the free market are valid for this sector as for any other, if there is a strike the deadlines for the completion of studies will be pushed back (if the research consultants do not make up for lost time, which would negate the meaning of their strike) and the company will be in a worse position to get contracts later on. On the other hand, it has a still greater responsibility vis-à-vis its permanent *financial underwriter,* which obviously will not be pleased by the "bad" functioning of the company it guarantees.

RESPONSIBILITY OR ALIENATION?

These unfair terms were the first thing the executives of the C.E.R.A.U. refused to tolerate. They were "fed up" with accepting this double tutelage as a natural fact and therefore challenged it. Upon reflection, they no longer quite understood why a given minister should take them for mere salesmen of services. The ministry gave money to make a study of the way in which the inhabitants of "X" view the reconstruction of the inner city demolished by the War. Why should the fact of paying for this research give the administration the "right of the buyer" as in the usual market relation? To whom does the money belong? Who provided it? The taxpayers! And the *Caisse des Déspots?* Who deposits money there, if not ordinary savers for the most part?

Let's take this a bit further. The executives are especially discontented because they do not have the feeling that their work is very useful. One of the commissions set up during the strike (which included occupation of the workplace) worked on the *goals* of the Research Bureaus. It came up with a brief description of the reasons for which certain studies were requested, and the later use to which they were put. It appeared that the great majority of studies and research serve less to inform a decision than as a "trump" in a dossier which one minister defends against another in discussions of a problem. Thus, the main function of science and reflection would be merely to contribute to the defense of positions in the internal debates of the administration!

This too is alienation. It is very hard for the researchers to find out what is done with a report once it is handed in; no doubt it will lie on some shelf alongside other prestigious discoveries. But *it suddenly seemed intolerable that the researcher have in the final analysis no control over the products of his own work.* Reports handed in are used in a tendentious manner, and this is justified in the name of a right of property held to be natural by the buyer: this is what a certain number of technicians challenged with more or less lucidity.

A STRIKE EXEMPLARY BY ITS LIMITS

The strike was exemplary because it was a nearly "pure" illustration of what a movement could represent today that linked the struggles of workers and students with those of executives, technicians and researchers. But it was also exemplary in a negative way, although full of things to learn on other points.

One point was solidarity with the May movement (moral and political but also financial solidarity: about one and a half million old francs were given to UNEF and to the Puteaux Inter-Union Council, and more recently to the C.L.E.O.P.); another point was the guilt of some researchers who felt they were "on the left" although they obviously profited from the social organization against which they struggled. And, finally, there was a very deeply felt unease in the face of the "dirty work" represented on the whole by this eminently ideological business of research bureaus.

Does this last point indicate at the same time why the strike movement is so limited in this sector? We are concerned here with people who actually want to change the present situation, and even to change it a lot. Do they have the means? Are they ready to appropriate them?

We have not yet spoken of the unions at the C.E.R.A.U. There are two union locals, CGT and CFDT. They are both recognized de facto by management and the most dynamic elements among the consultants and investigators are affiliated with them. They decide on the composition of the lists of nominees submitted to the personnel for the election of the company committee. A motion of the CGT union in Social Sciences can be read below. It came out at the beginning of the movement with the full support of the CGT local. This motion differs somewhat from the position of the Confederation. It shows that the role of the unions was not negligible, neither in terms of their position on the movement as a whole nor in terms of their real participation in the strike, including its initiation. But the union locals could do no more than to set up a unitary *Strike Committee* with some of the non-union employees. As a result, what was called "the *Action Committee*" ("out of solidarity!") was *really* representative, but that is also why the basic characteristics of the movement quickly became general moderation and latent corporatism. The movement was politically limited not because of the reasonable tone of the texts issued by its commissions, but because, in relation to their powerful protectors, research bureaus remain eminently dependent on the State, whatever its policies. It is at this level that the problem is posed.

Corporatism? The strike movement posed, we have said, purely internal problems of the company: management was not intransigent and moreover some levels of it participated in the general assemblies and the commissions. Satisfaction was granted on many points, in particular, time for Continuing Education during the work day, which means that one can pass the afternoon in the office Library, or read a recent book in one's own office—thus making official a practice which was obviously already ongoing! On others, the management of the firm could only raise its hands to the heavens: there were many things over which even *it* had no control! You talk to me about the self-management of the company, they said in substance, but as you well know that poses the problem of its finances: go reform the operating rules of the *Caisse des Dépots et Consignations!*

GETTING OUT OF THE RESEARCH BUREAUS

Would it have been possible to transcend this framework, that is to say, to formulate demands at a sufficiently general level so that all sorts of underlying issues which condition them might have been addressed? The solution was to be found in the first place at the level of a tighter link with the working class movement, especially in the Puteaux area: we have seen that contacts were made. The financial aid offered is a positive fact. But more positive still is a project to study *employment* in the Puteaux-Suresnes-Nanterre region for the Inter-Union Council under a contract with merely symbolic financial clauses (in other words, unpaid work). It would be unwise to predict the completion of this project, but let's hope that it gets going without too much delay. However, proposals for a more effective presence of the "technicians of urban affairs" among the local population have not yet been implemented: but this would require quite an effort of explanation concerning problems which both determine the framework of life and thought, and which are insoluble within a capitalist framework.

Another model of "opening onto the outside world" is to be found in several attempts at coordinating the various Research Bureaus. The result was disappointing. Meetings were held: energetic motions were voted in by about 30 Research Bureaus (among them the I.N.S.E.E., some services of the Ministry of National Education and of the C.N.R.S.). There too grass roots combativity was real, in spite of situations that were often quite difficult. Nearly everywhere two basic phenomena of the movement could be found: the very large number of executives on strike, hence the accent placed on general demands that were both politically interesting and practically somewhat abstract; on the other hand, everyone became aware of a very general convergence around one theme in nearly all the Research Bureaus and similar enterprises: *the status of the technician and the researcher.*

RESEARCH BUREAUS AND THE MIDDLE CLASS

Much remains to be said and perhaps this is not yet the time to say it. The result of these activities? For the moment, even now that the strike is over, what remains of the movement started at the C.E.R.A.U. is the very lively desire to retain a structure of permanent contacts to continue informational work on the general social situation. More deeply, a certain number of executives who both profit from a repressive society and are repressed by Profit Society, have become conscious of the fact that they were bringing the middle class into the fight for Socialism alongside the working class and the students. "Power is in the street!" It is not in the Research Bureaus but many were not convinced of this at first. Spreading this idea is perhaps the best way to incite researchers and technicians to place their work at the disposal of the only forces which can give their malaise a true anti-capitalist content.

Clearly, the example of the significance of May in the Research Bureaus poses the more general problem of the status of the middle class.

TWO DOCUMENTS[17]

The Declaration of the CGT Union of Social Sciences at the beginning of the Events.

The workers of the National Union of Social Sciences declare their intention to place their work in the service of the workers and not in the service of management and the capitalist State apparatus.

They offer their full solidarity to all the students and workers struggling against the present regime.

They warn against all demagogic attempts tending to discredit the student movement, in particular its most advanced elements, and to divide workers and students who are involved in a common struggle.

They gratefully salute those comrades, whether students or union members, who were victims of police repression in the course of the heroic struggles in the Latin Quarter, and who have begun a new phase in the process of contesting the regime.

They salute the workers who occupy their factories and their work places, whose ever growing struggle leads to decisive victories.

As workers they have the same aspirations as the working class as a whole: wages, working conditions, union and political freedoms.

They call on all workers in the Social Sciences to meet at their work places to examine their demands, to create Action Committees, and to determine the most effective methods of struggle, including striking and occupying the work place.

The National Union of Social Sciences calls on all its members to take the necessary measures to insure the success of this action.

---

17. The following documents were appended to this article by its authors.

The victorious conclusion of the movement is in the hands of the workers themselves, who must multiply attacks against the capitalist system.

The Motion of the First General Assembly
of the personnel of the C.E.R.A.U.

The General Assembly of the C.E.R.A.U., meeting May 21, 1968, goes on strike immediately to join the students and workers in the general movement of contestation.

This strike will occur at the workplace. The General Assembly of the personnel will meet daily to discuss the propositions of its commissions, charged with studying:

—other modes of participation in the movement,

—the self-management of the company,

—the critical analysis of the social and political role of its activities,

—wage, professional and structural demands appropriate to the company.

The General Assembly also declares its intention to obtain payment for the days of the strike and commits itself to contribute the amount received, less the SMIG,[18] to a strike fund the purpose of which will be defined later.

JOURNAL OF A NEIGHBORHOOD ACTION COMMITTEE

We publish here a report written collectively for the *Cahiers de Mai* by the members of the Maine-Montparnasse Neighborhood Action Committee.

---

18. The SMIG is the minimum wage.

On May 17, after the first events at the Sorbonne, three tenants in the Maine-Montparnasse complex invited a few students to come and explain their problems to the inhabitants of the building in the context of the "100 Meetings."[19] Our goal was a specific but rather narrow one: to contact the interested tenants and to decide together whether there was cause to form an Action Committee in our building.

This call brought out about twenty people on the terrace of our building. A discussion started but was quickly interrupted by a shower of projectiles from tenants who obviously did not want their terrace to be transformed into a forum. We were thus obliged to accept the hospitality of one of the organizers in order to continue safe from eggs, boiled potatoes and water bombs! This retreat was good for our discussion. We introduced ourselves: a photographer, an economist, a journalist, a psychologist, various executives, and we soon understood that each of us was already sensitized to the student problem and even to issues going well beyond it. During this first meeting we decided to form an Action Committee in our building and set the date for the first meeting in a room near our place.

THE STRIKE PICKET ASKS FOR HELP

This meeting revealed that around fifty people were willing to come at least for information and that many young people from the neighborhood were ready to participate actively in whatever the present gathering might decide to do.

From its inception, the Committee was oriented toward helping the strikers. Its activities took many forms and were especially concerned with the strikers at companies in the Maine-Montparnasse complex: the Postal Sorting Center, the Pullman Company, the construction site of the third sector and the Montparnasse railway station itself. It goes without saying that before May there had never been any contact between the workers and the tenants of Maine-Montparnasse.

The strike picket at the Mail Sorting Center had to guard very large premises with numerous entrances; although their numbers were sufficient they had a security problem. A telephone tree was devised: the strikers called four telephone numbers belonging to tenants in the build-

---

19. This complex consists of several gigantic modern buildings in the south of Paris that stand out like a sore thumb of modern urbanism in the midst of the old city.

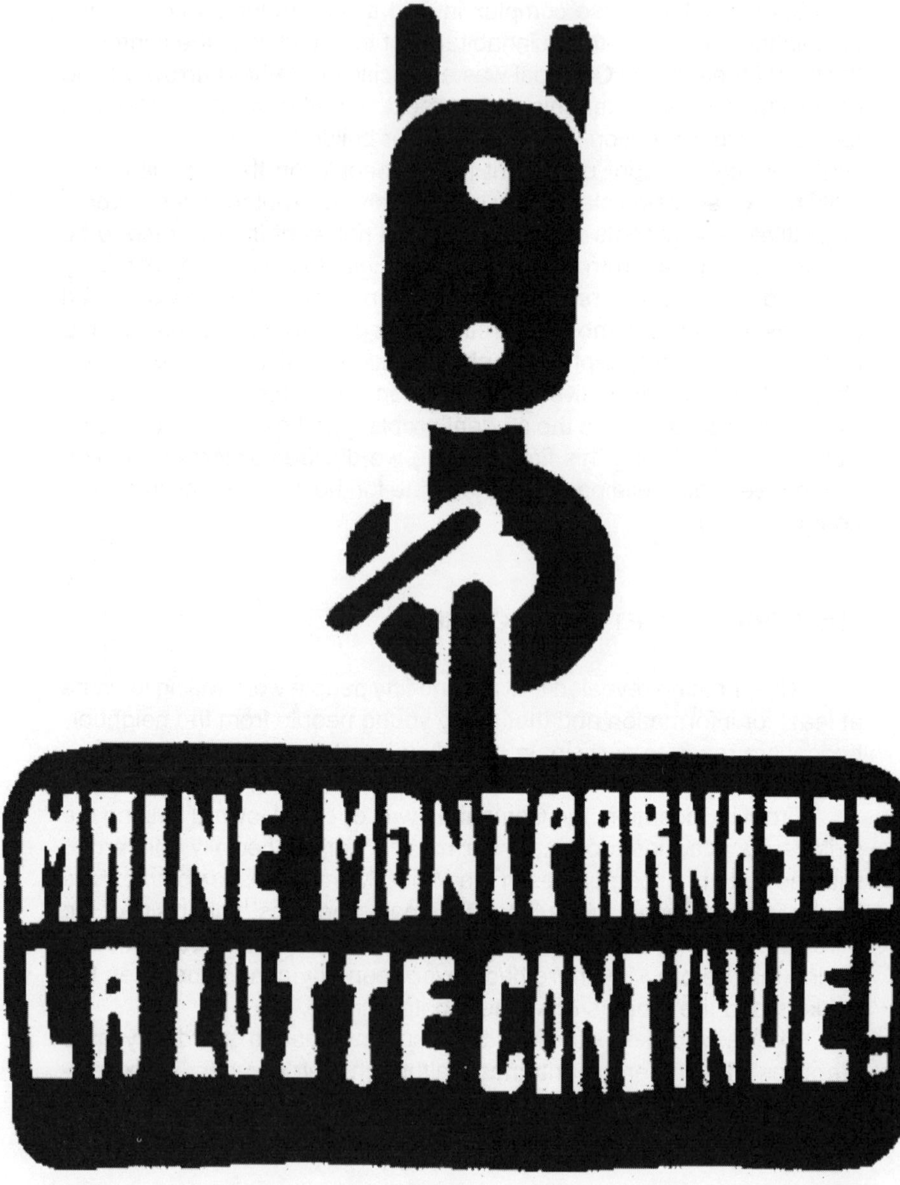
MAINE MONTPARNASSE
LA LUTTE CONTINUE!

ing and these latter called four others, etc. Thus in an emergency we could contact the maximum people in a minimum of time (seven minutes). We had an opportunity to test the effectiveness of this system when the "fascists" came to "say hello" to the strikers. But as soon as they saw us they fled, understanding clearly what was going to happen to them! Also, every night four or five members of the Committee waited for dawn with the strikers. It was more a question of maintaining their morale than of offering material aid.

Relations with the strikers of the construction site were different. The strike picket we contacted answered that they had no special problems but that they would be happy to have coffee at night! So, every night we brought them bottles of coffee. Of course we rotated the task because they needed the coffee around midnight when the night really begins.

THE PARTIAL RETURN TO WORK DOES NOT STOP OUR STRUGGLE

Then on Tuesday, June 5, new problems arose: new supplies of gas having arrived the preceding weekend (Pentecost), the government announced the general return to work. The building construction union had not reached an agreement with management; the companies of the Maine-Montparnasse construction site announced the re-opening for Tuesday morning. The strike picket asked for our help: their strikers were not numerous enough to take on those who would want to return to work. They wanted many of us to come, not to stop workers from entering the construction site, but to talk with them to try to show them that the strike will have been wasted if they go back to work before an agreement has been reached. For our part, we asked for reinforcements from the other committees in the 14th District, from the extreme left organizations in the area, and from occasional students we had met. From 70 to 100 people were at the construction site at six in the morning: there were almost as many workers (mostly foreigners) as agents of management and foremen. The Strike Committee gave no instructions, everyone argued amongst themselves and the confusion was total. We did not know whether to block the entrance to the construction site or not. It seemed awkward for us, an Action Committee, to make such a move.

After two hours, management got the workers into the construction site (which was closed to us) and organized a vote (that was more than slightly fixed) in favor of the return to work. The vote was by so-called "secret ballot" and not by raised hands; in fact an employee of management went around with a notebook and asked each worker individually whether he was for the return to work! He noted down something for each answer. The return to work won! 100 voters for a thousand workers! Sixty percent in favor of the return to work, essentially executives and branch heads! And dozens of foreign workers who do not understand our language, who do not know what they are asked and who, in any case, know that they may be deported for their answer. However, when it was explained to them that they had answered "yes" to the return to work, they went and asked the organizers of the "vote" to annul their answer. "Too late," they were told, "you have voted."

We could not intervene in any way; that would have given the bosses an opportunity to call the police and to expel those who did not belong on the construction site. The police came anyway, called by an inhabitant of the Avenue de Maine who was afraid of fights! Helmets, billy clubs, tear gas were supposed to make "everyone" reasonable again. In fact, young people were asked more or less rudely to move on.

Of the twenty or so companies which participated in the construction work, only two had union representation. In the others the workers, most of them foreigners, went on strike to follow "the movement" while hoping to benefit from it. They went on strike for two weeks without even presenting a list of demands and without having established intercompany contacts. Very quickly, in a neighboring café, around fifteen workers wrote up a leaflet with us affirming the solidarity of all the companies on the construction site, presenting demands, and asking the workers to discuss them freely before returning to work. Lacking means to print the leaflet, our comrades from the construction site asked us to do it for them and to come back the following day to help with distribution.

On the practical level our action met with failure, since in the end management got what it wanted. But we contributed to a beginning of awareness and organization among the workers of Maine-Montparnasse. It is a good question why no more established organization than our committee had thought of doing this.

UNION DELEGATES AND PULLMAN WORKERS

The relations between the Pullman employees and our committee were fraternal, but they did not ask us for practical aid. And so we discussed the Events daily and went on little "sorties": for instance, one day we went and removed the posters which an ad agency put up for the incumbent deputy from "la Maléne" and, in order to re-establish a certain balance in the decoration of the neighborhood, we put up posters from the Peoples' Studio about our committee or the companies of Maine-Montparnasse.

We had a few problems with the Montparnasse railroad station itself. From the inception of our committee, we went to see the railway workers' strike picket to offer it our services. We were very well received and our position understood, but since no union leaders were present the railway comrades advised us to go to see them at neighborhood inter-union headquarters. There we were extremely ill received! Apparently the "leaders" took us for organized "ultra-leftists" and we were therefore welcomed as is fitting in such cases! Unfortunately, one of the members of the committee who went to the inter-union headquarters was a communist known as such by the union leaders, and so relations deteriorated. The railwaymen let us know through one of their leaders that they did not wish to establish contacts with us. We nevertheless understood that the aforesaid leader spoke only in his own name.

A DIFFICULT TRANSITION: FROM STRIKES TO ELECTIONS

During the period when strike support constituted our main activity, we rarely asked basic questions. But this changed as soon as the elections became certain. Our Action Committee is composed of members who have in common their district, their good will and their leftist ideas. We are more or less aware that some of us belong to the Communist Party, to the P.S.U., to organizations such as U.J.C.M.L., or the J.C.R., the anarcho-syndicalists, while others are members of the CGT, or simply non-affiliated and unpoliticized, but no one ever tries to impose the point of view of his organization on the Committee. On the contrary, everyone is free and engages in spontaneous discussion during the writing up of a leaflet, the creation of a poster, or the organization of a meeting. In the weekly discussions we organize, compromises are rare and a common line of action stands out clearly.

The preparation for the elections created some dissension. It turned out that the majority was for abstention, but only the majority! We discussed this at length but, as ever, action united us. Perhaps the best proof was the meetings we held in the neighborhood as often as possible. There, whether each of us was for or against the elections, we all knew how to explain what they represented in the framework of the present Constitution with its system of voting. In this regard, it is worth stressing the success of these meetings. It was so great that when we cannot organize a meeting in the usual places, the residents of the neighborhood show up alone to talk. Later they ask us in the street why we did not come, what is happening now, etc.

NEW WAYS OF COMMUNICATING: MEETINGS IN THE STREET

We decided to have a bulletin board to broaden our means of communication. We posted articles from the daily press, from *Action*, leaflets, documents and photographs of the events at the Edgar Quinet market as well as at the exit of the Montparnasse subway station in front of the movie theater.

As experience showed again and again, discussions started thanks to people who insulted us, and then others came to our rescue and things really got going! It was impossible to hold just one discussion and numerous groups formed on different subjects: history, current events, politics, intellectual and union affairs, social problems, etc. It is hard to classify the hundred or so people who participate each time in our discussions. There is a bit of everything. In the first place we are there, overwhelmed by the crowd but also helped by passersby. Each group, from three to six people, is led by those who are most directly concerned by one of these problems. Examination of contemporary events interests those who are younger and more middle class. They tend to agree with the student demands (which are their children's), and are easily led on to social problems. History is generally of interest to Gaullists or members of the extreme right who try to justify themselves; we have been astonished to hear the name of Pétain, who still attracts sympathy: "It was thanks to Pétain that the Resistance could exist!"[20] The various unions are, of course, analyzed by the workers who all agree on the ambiguous role of the CGT, but not on how to lead or end the strike.

And then there are the old people. There are two kinds: those who say they are satisfied with their lot and who answer, when asked if they could manage in case of serious illness, "Oh well, if you ask questions

---

20. Pétain was the chief military leader of France in World War I, and in his old age accepted the political leadership of defeated France in World War II. He briefly ruled a rump French republic in alliance with Germany from the town of Vichy. After the War he was condemned to life imprisonment for treason.

like that," or "We are old, we hardly need anything"; and those who astonish us with their political ideas and their revolutionary force (especially the women). After a long discussion on socialism in France, an old woman concluded with a smile: "The only thing I'm still skeptical about is the possibility of changing man!"

Every day of course new themes are discussed, but the following question is always posed: "With what do you propose to replace the present government?" After having explained that our final goal is still the abolition of private ownership of the means of production, we underline our original position with respect to changes in government. By contrast with the traditional political parties, we propose no personality, no tendency. Unlike these parties we as an Action Committee do not want to discuss possible solutions with anyone who has vested political interests (precisely these parties). With this answer we hope to communicate that this problem concerns each of us.

THE RELATIONS WITH ORGANIZED MOVEMENTS

Politically, our Action Committee has no defined ideology. When we agree with the instructions of the Coordination Committee of the Sorbonne, or the Rue Serpente, we carry them out; thus, we participated in all the demonstrations organized by UNEF and the S.N.E.Sup. (to the great surprise of the tenants of Maine-Montparnasse who were astonished to see a group of demonstrators, led by a red flag, lining up in their building). We are truly autonomous with respect to all organizations of students, young people or others. The only disputes we have are little fights over posters with the Communist Party and over "zones of influence" in the neighborhood.

There is in fact a center for 14th District Action Committees where material is organized and distributed. The other Action Committees of the district are not formed on the same recruiting base as ours; there is a March 22 Action Committee, and an Action Committee of the U.J.C.M.L. (*Union des Jeunesses Communiste, Marxiste-Léniniste,* a Maoist sect). For instance, a common demonstration was decided upon, limited just to our district. We were to go around to the local companies and show our solidarity. The Maine-Montparnasse Committee arrived in large numbers, but we could tell right away that this demonstration was more representative of the U.J.C.M.L. than of the Fourteenth District Action Committees in terms of the slogans, press, leaflets, and participants (who, even if they did not all live in the neighborhood, belonged to the

U.J.C.M.L.) One part of our Action Committee left the demonstration for that reason while the other half remained for the sake of unity, but this explains why our participation was not all that positive. We were rather ill-received by the companies in our neighborhood! Indeed, long nocturnal discussions with strikers had finally convinced them that we belonged to no political group (especially those against which the CGT union delegates were struggling) and our participation in that demonstration showed the contrary; the comrades of our Action Committee had a hard time reestablishing good relations with the strikers. We want to stress that these little problems of relations with organized movements are not ideological but purely tactical. It is, incidentally, amusing to see the members of our Action Committee serve as intermediaries between ourselves and the political organizations to which they belong. It really facilitates relations!

But after that demonstration on June 3, we have been taking care that the leaflets we receive from the 14th District Center, signed by the Action Committee of the 14th, are not excessively oriented towards denunciation or abstentionism. We just want any leaflet like that to be distributed with a signature and thus to be the responsibility of the Action Committee that wrote it.

The Maine-Montparnasse complex is a good illustration of "segregated" urbanism: total segregation inscribed in the very conception of the building, in the walls and the elevators; separation between the offices, between the workplaces and the inhabitants; separation between the "new" and the old quarter; separation between the apartments within the building itself. They are all comfortable (and expensive!) but there are no places for social life, no playground for children.

May 1968 has been stronger than the walls. All these separations have broken down; tenants and workers in the complex and inhabitants of other streets in the neighborhood have finally started to struggle together, to get to know each other, to become friends. The Committee has become one of the public realities of the neighborhood, through its posters, its small meetings, the distribution of *Action* and the *Cahiers de Mai,* its leaflets and demonstrations.

Two examples show this:

—on the evening of the Gaullist demonstration on the Champs-Elysées, a Gaullist tenant tried to show off his power in the building by hanging a *tricolore* flag with a Lorraine Cross in his window. No doubt he was unaware of the size of our Action Committee, for his weapon turned against him when the immense facade of Maine-Montparnasse was covered with red flags (slacks, sweaters, table cloths, the red part of the *tricolore,* etc). Without the Action Committee, no tenant would have dared to believe in such an exhibition of red; it was our first victory.

—despite the difficulty of raising hard cash, our campaign brought in a little more than 2000 Francs. Indeed, people have confidence in us for they know us and they give more easily to us than to strangers. We brought this sum to the strikers at the mail sorting office for them to distribute among the different companies on strike, but they informed us immediately that their strikers were not in urgent need and they proposed to give it to Renault. And so it was done.

THE NEXT CHAPTER REMAINS TO BE WRITTEN . . .

The next chapter is not yet written, we are living it (internal economic questions, political discussions, education, library, invitations to specialists, meetings, etc. . . .) with all the others in the factories, in the universities, in the neighborhoods; we are carrying on the movement.

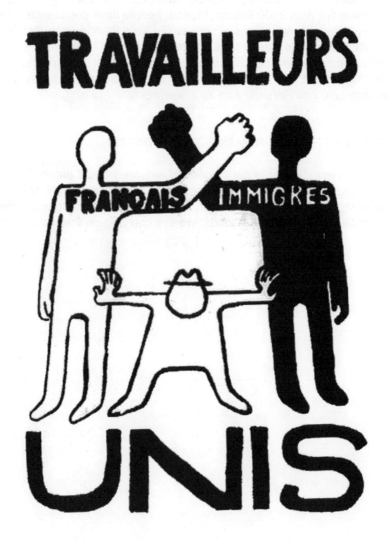

TRAVAILLEURS

FRANÇAIS IMMIGRES

UNIS

Essay III. The Worker-Student Alliance

"Freedom is the crime which contains all crimes. It is our ultimate weapon."[21]

In a society that pretends to be based on knowledge, revolt in the university is a refutation of all the claims of the social hierarchy. It shows that there is something profoundly wrong in the citadel of knowledge itself. Insofar as the university is understood ideologically as a model of the society, student revolt can appear to students to be the model for generalized revolution.

But for revolution actually to occur, the model-reality relations experienced in the university must be reversed. Students could universalize their movement because the university was already identified in their minds as a universal metaphor to the society. But for others outside the university to understand the significance of the student movement and join its struggle in solidarity, they had to perceive its similarity to their own situation. This was the purpose of much student propaganda, which described the student movement on the model of a

---

21. Graffiti from the walls of Paris during the May Events. "D'Où Vient la Violence," published by the Jeunesse Communiste Révolutionnaire in early May. "Camarades Ouvriers" published by the Comité d'Action Ouvriers-Etudiants around May 15. "Votre Lutte est la Notre," May 24, Mouvement du 22 Mars. Graffiti from the walls of Paris during the May Events. "Vers une Gauchisme de Masse," June 7, Jeunesse Communiste Révolutionnaire. "La CFDT S'Addresse aux Travailleurs," May 18, the CFDT.

classic revolutionary uprising in order to make it an example for the whole society.[22]

The labor movement provided the dominant metaphor in terms of which the French students described their struggle. This choice flowed both from a realistic sense of the limitations of an isolated student revolt, and from the prestige of traditional Left ideology. Thus leaflets like the following one were widely distributed in the first days of the movement to justify its violence to workers and to provoke them to violence as well.

WORKERS,

—You too are forced to struggle to defend your gains against government attacks.

—You too have encountered the CRS and the Mobile Guards, come to break your resistance.

—You too have been slandered by the Boss's press and by the government Radio.

You know that violence is in the nature of the existing social order. You know that it strikes down those who dare to challenge it: the batons of the CRS answered our demands, just as the rifle butts of the Mobile Guards answered the workers of Caen, Redon and Mans.

Soon student leaflets began to draw the parallel between student and labor demands: "Between your problems and ours there are certain similarities: jobs and opportunities, standards and work pace, union rights, self-management."

The factory occupations that quickly followed showed the reciprocity of the model-reality relation: they were coded simultaneously in terms of the student occupation of the Sorbonne, begun on May 13, and similar factory occupations in 1936, which latter could themselves be described as the model for the students' actions. One leaflet that was widely distributed to workers was entitled "Your Struggle Is Ours!" In it the students said, "Your struggle and our struggle converge. Everything which isolates the one from the other (habit, the newspapers, etc.) must be destroyed. We must link up the occupied factories and the campuses."

---

22. For a more elaborate discussion of the relations between workers and students, see the similar analysis of Vidal in P. Dubois et al. *Grèves Revendicatives ou Grèves Politiques?* (Paris: Anthropos, 1971).

How successful was this strategy? The French student revolt provoked a general strike by millions of workers. The strikers seized hundreds of factories all over the country, paralyzing commerce and transportation for over a month. The government was largely helpless as well, and only the police and professional army actively supported the tottering state.

Yet it is difficult to gauge labor support for the actual goals of the student movement. The students had little influence on the major working-class organizations such as the Communist Party and the CGT. Continuing for the most part to confine the union struggle to wages and working conditions and the political struggle to the forging of electoral alliances, the Party completely misunderstood what was new about the movement: its demand for a transformation of daily life and culture and its emphasis on workers' power on the workplace. As a result, the communists found the new student opposition contesting their own leadership of the working class from the left.

The communists counterattacked by charging the students with "*gauchisme*"—ultraleftism, to which the students responded by accusing the Party of another equally serious deviation, "opportunism." The stale insults had flown back and forth for years, but unlike earlier struggles between French communists and "*gauchistes*," this time the students broke out of the traditional isolation of the old anarchist, Trotskyist, and Maoist sects; never before had such a profound social crisis been orchestrated against the will of such a strong Communist Party.

In a leaflet entitled "Toward a Mass Leftism," a Trotskyist group commented: "The role fulfilled by the '*gauchistes*' was, within certain limits, that which an authentically revolutionary leadership would have played: foreseeing the course of the movement (and this is not a question of dates), organizing it, directing it." That such results could have been achieved shows that the communists had disastrously underestimated the political consciousness of the workers they were attempting to lead.

The second largest union federation, the CFDT, was drawn into the movement, adopted the symbols and goals proposed by the students, at least verbally, and pushed for a strategy of structural reforms far to the left of anything demanded by the communists. In a major leaflet distributed by the CFDT on May 18, this organization addressed workers with an interpretation of the movement similar to that of the students.

The intolerable constraints and structures against which the students rose exist similarly, and still more intolerably, in the factories, construction sites, and offices. . . .

The government yielded to the students. To freedom in the university must correspond freedom in the factories. Democratic structures based on self-management must be substituted for industrial and administrative monarchy.

The Moment Has Come To Act.

Despite this verbal support, student activists decided to appeal over the heads of the unions directly to the workers. To a certain extent they were successful, although they could not overcome in a few weeks the effects of years of mutual ignorance. In any case the students were encouraged to try by the massive strike that began independent of the parties and unions; by the rejection of the communist supported *Accords de Grenelle*, negotiated by the unions to settle the strike; by the brief radicalization of the Communist Party at the end of May when, under pressure from the grass roots, it demanded de Gaulle's resignation; and by the appearance of a significant minority of revolutionary workers at the Sorbonne, on the barricades, in factory and union meetings.

In fact, two groups of workers were deeply influenced by the student strategy, and it was their opposition to ending the strike and their participation in the street fighting that makes it possible to speak of a real worker-student alliance during May. The first of these two groups was the technicians, particularly those organized by the CFDT, which over the years had become their chief representative. The idea of self-management had more immediate appeal to these workers than to any others. They were highly trained and felt competent to run the factories in which they were employed. The CFDT had responded to this sentiment long before the May Events by demanding a share in management.[23]

Young workers were drawn to the students for other reasons. They proved to be tremendously combative and impatient for revolution. Many of them joined the students on the barricades and fought the police. They served on worker-student coordinating committees and

---

23. The classic discussion in the French literature of the attitudes of technicians is Serge Mallet, *La Nouvelle Classe Ouvrière* (Paris: Seuil, 1963). Later Mallet argued that the May Events confirmed his approach in *Le Pouvoir Ouvrier* (Paris: Anthropos, 1971).

influenced student thinking about workers while being influenced in their turn. In some cases they were inspired by the Events to join one or another of the Maoist and Trotskyist *groupuscules* that flourished at that time.

These young workers argued for violent and immediate revolution, sometimes in a way that indicated contempt or condescension toward older workers and the Party for having failed to do the job in the past. Many older workers, they seemed to feel, had resigned themselves but they had no intention of following in their fathers' footsteps; they were not going to "swallow" defeats and humiliations without making their try for freedom, whatever wiser heads from the unions might advise.

Parallel phenomena occurred in the following two years among young workers in Italy, particularly those of southern origin. They were even less integrated into established union and party organizations than their French counterparts, a factor that seems directly related to their intense combativity. Often first-generation immigrants to the cities, with no proletarian roots at all, they unhesitatingly attacked structures and practices that seemed "natural" to the older or more urbanized workers. In Italy this included the entire organization of manual labor: systems of piecework, the assembly line, the wage hierarchy, pay supplements for dangerous work, and so on.

A few years later rather similar struggles occurred in the United States, the most famous of which was the Lordstown strike of 1971–1972. There too, young workers dissatisfied less with the rewards than the servitudes of industrial labor made a new kind of strike indicative of profound changes in the expectations of workers in advanced capitalist societies.[24]

The New Left was thus not exclusively a student affair. Industrial workers, who were believed to be content with receiving periodic wage increases, also came forward in this period with demands for power and control over the work process. In France such struggles dovetailed with the attack on the organization of labor from above begun by the students and supported by many employees in the professions and the bureaucracies.[25]

---

24. Stanley Aronowitz, *False Promises.* (New York: McGraw-Hill, 1973), chap. 2.

25. The importance of the aspiration for power in the May Events is supported by statistical evidence in an article by Melvin Seeman, "The Signals of '68: Alienation in Pre-Crisis France," *American Sociological Review,* 1972, Volume 37, no. 4, p. 399.

The Texts

"The Students at Flins."   The struggle between workers, students, and police for possession of the Renault factory at Flins in early June was one of the most violent episodes of the Events. At this time both the Communist Party and the government were anxious to terminate the strikes in order to transfer the battle to the electoral plane. But the Flins workers wanted to fight on and they succeeded in defeating the back-to-work strategy in their workplace. Four days after the police takeover of their factory, the workers were back in control and a week later Renault's management offered huge concessions to end the strike. This article recounts the beginning of the violence at Flins, and defends the movement against the charges of the communists and the government. The article appeared in *Les Cahiers de Mai,* no. 3, August–September 1968.

"The People's Studio."   During the May Events, thousands of posters appeared all over France, glued to the walls of buildings and recounting the slogans and struggles of the day. Many of them are reproduced in this book. The famous Ecole des Beaux Arts in Paris was the factory in which these posters were made. This article describes how the students and artists organized themselves to contribute their skills to the movement. The article is taken from *Les Cahiers de Mai,* no. 2, July, 1968.

THE STUDENTS AT FLINS

THE NIGHT OF THE SIXTH OF JUNE AND THE MORNING OF THE SEVENTH

The presence of students from Paris in front of the Flins Renault factory on the seventh of June at dawn inspired a whole literature (of the mystery and spy type). On one side we are shown calm and disciplined workers led by wise leaders with a sense of responsibility, and on the other side bizarre and shady characters who suddenly appear from all

**MANIFESTATION GARE DE L'EST
MARDI 11 A 19 H**

over in obedience to mysterious instructions, determined to stir up trouble against the will of the workers.

It is therefore interesting to know why and how the students came to be in front of the Flins factory on June 7 from 5:00 in the morning on. Who called for them? And what role did they play?

As everyone is aware, the Flins Renault factory is situated in the middle of the countryside, between Mantes (l2 km.) and Les Mureaux (5 km.) in the Seine-et-Oise Department. On the one side the Seine river flows, the freeway and the railroad are on the other side. Cars are produced there (R4, R8, R10, Rl6) with engines from the Cléon factory, 19 km. south of Rouen. Ten thousand five hundred workers are employed at Flins and live scattered over the region. Most of them arrive and leave at the Les Mureaux railroad station, where the Renault company runs a bus service. Some of them own a private vehicle and arrive directly. The workers are called—or at least before May and June they were called—the "beet farmers" because there are beets around the factory, and especially because many workers arrived straight from the provinces or even from the farm. They became workers only recently. There are also many foreigners among them—Spaniards, Portuguese, Yugoslavs. Also blacks. Before the strike, only 7 percent of the Flins workers belonged to the CGT or the CFDT (today it's around 15 percent) but this did not stop the factory from going on strike from May 17 on, the day after the beginning of the strike and occupation at Cléon.

THE LOCAL SITUATION, THURSDAY AFTERNOON

Three weeks later, on Thursday, June 6, at 3:00 A.M., about 1000 CRS and Mobile Guards surrounded the factory and, using bulldozers, overturned the barricades the strike picket put up at night and the campfire around which it kept warm. The strike picket was chased away from the factory. Then, in the morning, management announced that, since the forces of order had restored the "right to work" at Flins, the workers should report back on the next day, Friday, June 7.

As soon as the news of the Flins occupation became known—i.e., on the morning of June 6—many workers gathered around the factory and a demonstration went through neighboring communities in the afternoon, calling for a continuation of the strike. For their part, the student and teacher organizations participating in the May movement proposed a "march on Flins" in support of the struggling workers.

But a communique, prematurely signed by the Renault CGT Union, declared:

> The Gaullist government and M. Dreyfus have suffered a stinging defeat in trying to force the return to work in the Flins factory. The mass of workers continues the strike in all the Renault factories. We demand the immediate departure of all police from Flins.
>
> On the other hand, we have heard that the leaders of the student and teacher unions have decided to call for a march on Flins. We want to clearly signify our total disagreement with such an initiative, which risks favoring a police provocation and harming the Renault workers' strike.
>
> The Flins workers, like those of Billancourt, have shown their ability to solve their own problems in ways decided upon by the workers and in their own interests.

This communique, dated June 6, thus announces *24 hours in advance* that the attempt to force the return to work at Flins will fail, since the struggle for or against the return to work was to take place only on the morning of June 7. The goal seemed to be to dissuade the students from going to Flins by making them believe that all was well and that anyway, they would arrive after the struggle was over.

But the Flins workers themselves—those who wanted to continue the struggle—began to worry about the decisions of the CGT and the CFDT on the local level. The only response from the union leaders to the occupation of the factory was to call a meeting at Les Mureaux (that is, 5 km. away from the factory) for the following day on June 7 at 8:00 in the morning. However, all the workers were well aware that the first shift (1500) began work at 5:30 A.M. and the second shift (6000) at 7:30 A.M. To whom was this call for a meeting addressed? Without clear instructions, not knowing whether the strike continued or not, wouldn't numerous workers and especially the foreigners, climb into the buses and go back to work when management turned on the heat? And at 8:00, when the meeting would begin in the presence of a minority of workers, wouldn't the strike really be over already, and wouldn't the workers meeting at Les Mureaux be placed before the accomplished fact?

THE WORKERS AT THE ART SCHOOL

Late Thursday, June 6, a few workers from Flins arrived at the Ecole des Beaux Arts. Many organizations had retreated there after the occupation of various university facilities by the police, including the Coordinating Committee of the Action Committees, the Committee for Support for the Peoples Struggles, The March 22 Movement, as well as the Peoples Studio whose posters are well known and greatly appreciated by numerous workers. They explained the situation to the students—in particular the question of the shifts and the topography of the place—and they asked for help.

Their reasoning was logical: the inter-union meeting at Les Mureaux at 8:00 is senseless—unless it is an attempt to sabotage the strike. What is needed is another picket line in front of the factory, from 5:00 in the morning on. The population and the students must be asked to join this picket line. First of all, could the students print a leaflet?

But the students did not want to rush into action without sizing up the situation on the spot. They designated someone to go to Les Mureaux. He left immediately in a young worker's car.

"During the trip," the student recalled, "he seemed very tense and asked me specifically about the tear gas grenades, but with some embarrassment, without insisting. He said: 'What is it like? What does it do exactly? Do they shoot them from far off or what? . . . ' All these questions implied that we, the students, already knew the score, were already experienced. He also said: 'Tomorrow will be a big day! There's going to be some action. . . . ' But he was still shocked by the arrival of the cops. He did not seem to be afraid. Just touched by something new to him. He also told me about his wife. He had to go home before the others because of her. She was waiting for him. She was not happy to see him mixed up in all this. 'Even though I explain to her that it's to defend our bread! But she doesn't want to hear anything about it. . . . ' So he let me off in front of the Les Mureaux railway station where they were waiting for us, and he went home because of his wife. But the following morning, from 5:00 A.M. on, I found him again in front of the factory, neatly combed and shaven.

"At the Les Mureaux railway station, I found about 50 young workers. Jackets, long hair, a scarf around their necks, and CGT emblems in their lapels. They told me they intended to hold a meeting in front of the factory doors before the arrival of the first shift. They wanted a leaflet right away. 'A very simple one,' they said. 'No bull.' So we wrote up the leaflet without wasting time, and called the text in to the Art School from a nearby café. It was full of people who were discussing politics, all very excited. I hesitated a little because the telephone was right in the open. But then I decided to go ahead, what the hell! The owner and the clients heard everything. It lasted a rather long time . . . and then when I asked for the price of the call to Paris, the owner looked at his meter, and hesitated. Finally, he said 50 centimes (10 cents), just to have me pay a token amount, and he added proudly: 'My telephone was good for something! . . .'"

Ten thousand copies of the leaflet were published. As soon as they were ready, cars brought them to Les Mureaux in the evening with a few other students, who formed mixed worker-student teams to distribute them in a perimeter of about 15 km.

The leaflet read:

GENERAL MOBILIZATION
workers-students
In response to the occupation of their factory by 6000 CRS, the Renault Flins workers ask all available workers and students to meet
JUNE 7 AT 5:00 IN THE MORNING
Place de l'Etoile at ELISABETHVILLE.
(near the Flins factory)
TO MASSIVELY DEMONSTRATE THEIR SUPPORT!
The workers of Renault-Flins

"But it was after midnight. People were sleeping. At Mantes in the public housing project, we shoved the leaflets under the doors and rang the bell, without waiting for the people to open. We hoped to wake them up. All this unfortunately, was not very effective. Most people would find the leaflet on waking up, that is to say, after 5:00. . . ."

IN FRONT OF THE FACTORY, 5:30 A.M. AND THE ARRIVAL OF THE FIRST SHIFT

After the distribution of the leaflet, the mixed teams returned to the Les Mureaux railway station, where other workers and students arrived little by little from the Paris region. They slept for an hour or two in the waiting room or in cars, and around 4:00 in the morning, they began to leave for the factory by the back roads. Around 5:00 they finally sat down on the road in front of the police cordon which blocked the factory entrance. Two or three cars with students came directly from Paris. But when the first shift began to arrive, there was still only one picket line in front of the factory, consisting of l00 to 150 people two thirds of whom were Flins workers and one third students. Moreover, no union leader had showed up. Nevertheless, the picket grew steadily because the vast majority of the workers who arrived (the first ones by private means of transportation) unhesitatingly joined the initial group. Then the buses with the first shift arrived. The Mobile Guards, which had remained in front of the factory, advanced to clear the road and pushed the strike picket back on the other side of the road, towards the Place de l'Etoile in Elisabethville. But the workers got out of the buses and instead of going towards the factory, crossed the road and also joined their comrades. In short, there was no problem with the first shift.

But the battle was not won. Management no doubt counted on the six thousand workers of the second shift to impose the return to work. But after this first success, the strikers and students were gaining confidence. Nevertheless, we kept looking down the road while waiting for the buses. We made fun of the outfits of the Mobile Guards and the CRS. This was the first time most workers saw their shields and visors. The students were surrounded as they proudly explained how to protect oneself from the gases used by the police. It was around 7:00. Cars full of students continued to arrive. One of them even carried a trunk on its roof from which the newcomers pulled motorcycle helmets and sticks. Among all the facts mentioned by observers, this is the only detail that could support the assertion that the students were "quasi-militarily trained units." All in all, this is not much in the way of organization after a month of police brutality. As far as the "quasi-military" character of this team was concerned, it was not really obvious. Who has ever heard of soldiers going out on an operation with their helmets and weapons locked in a trunk on the roof of their vehicle! Nevertheless, the new arrivals were asked by their student comrades not to wear their helmets nor to brandish their sticks. Many young workers had the same reflex of self-defense and hid their clubs. For all, without exception, the real provocation was the presence of Mobile Guards and CRS at Flins.

However, at that moment, the atmosphere was more a sort of vengeful gaiety. An amusing scene took place along the road involving the Prefect of the Department, a tall clumsy fellow who had put on his uniform for the occasion. Surrounded by a dozen very pale local policemen, he too tried to chase the young workers and students off the road. "Move back! Move back!" he shouted. "Respect the right to work!" And as he passed, he was followed by shouts and especially by laughter. From all sides were heard cries of: "Ridiculous! Comic! Clown!" Someone even poked a finger in his back. He turned around, furious: "Who did that! I want to know who did that! . . ." Then someone else suddenly took his arm and spun him around three times, no doubt as a sign of contempt. The local policemen did not intervene—they grew paler and paler—and the Prefect disappeared.

7:30 A.M., THE SECOND SHIFT

Then an uninterrupted line of buses full of workers was seen moving up the road, a line that seemed to stretch over several kilometers. This was the second shift. The CRS evacuated the other side of the road, pushing the strikers and the students further and further back in the direction of the Place de l'Etoile in Elisabethville. But young workers and students overflowed the CRS cordon on its left, slid along the road, and stood in front of the buses, forcing them to stop. They went inside the buses and told the workers: "The cops hold the factory. You cannot return to work with a gun in your back! The strike isn't over. . . ." Many workers got out of the buses immediately, while those who remained seated inside were insulted. But other buses did get to the factory. Some workers went in at first, and then came out again. But most buses were stopped on the road in spite of the CRS, who tried to drive alongside the line of buses in their small vehicles, chasing the young workers and students toward the shoulders of the road.

Meanwhile, three CGT leaders finally arrived. They stood on the railroad embankment and shouted through megaphones from afar: "Comrades, the strike continues! But no provocation! No provocation! . . . " At times they made fun of the students when the latter, like the workers who were with them along the road, were pushed back by the CRS to the foot of the embankment.

MEANWHILE, AT LES MUREAUX

It was now 8:00. Approximately 80 to 90 percent of the second shift did not enter the factory. Moreover, workers who at first went in were constantly leaving in groups to the applause of the strikers and the students. But what happened at Les Mureaux where the inter-union meeting had been arranged?

"To my great surprise," a student said, "the meeting still had not been called off. The union representatives were there, on the steps of the city hall with their loudspeaker and there were at most two or three hundred workers listening to them. A representative of the CFDT spoke first. He seemed rather embarrassed. I only remember that he said: 'The situation is unclear. It is in flux, comrades. It evolves all the time, comrades. . . .' But someone behind him pulled him by the sleeve to ask him to stop. He agreed and someone came to announce that the meeting was moved to the Place de l'Etoile in Elisabethville, just as it had been announced on the leaflet which we had made at the request of the young workers! Admittedly, the union representatives were three hours late. . . "

RETURN TO ELISABETHVILLE

The loudspeaker and the union leaders thus arrived at the Place de l'Etoile at Elisabethville and there they went up onto a platform situated in the middle of the square. Around them there were at least seven thousand workers from Flins plus a few hundred students. Jean Breteau, the General Secretary of the Metal Workers Federation (CGT), began to speak. He assured the Flins workers of the solidarity of all the other metal workers, especially those of Billancourt, which got thundering applause. He read telegrams from foreign countries and thanked "the students who have come from Paris to support the Flins workers." He added that "collaboration requires the presence of numerous students but that the workers have the exclusive leadership of their own struggle." Then, after asking for the withdrawal of the police, he announced that a delegation would be going immediately to meet with the management of the factory.

A representative from the CFDT then spoke. He too thanked "the student comrades who pursue one and the same struggle with the workers." They were the first, he says, to climb into the buses to explain to the workers that they should not go back to work.

The meeting was over—at least in the minds of the union leaders. But a clamor rose up from the mass of workers: "Let the students speak." One of them, standing near the War Memorial, was pushed toward the microphone. The CGT representatives did not want to give it to him. They even began to unplug the sound system. The workers who witnessed the scene immediately protested, and behind them, their comrades pushed the students forward so that they could speak. One could hear among other things: "You're not going to oppose the will of the rank and file, are you? Are you managers or representatives?" A scuffle broke out. A union representative finally gave the microphone to a student. He declared that, "The students have come from Paris to support the workers who want to take their factory back from the cops. . . ." He expressed himself clumsily. But Alain Geismar, who arrived at Flins around 6 A.M., then spoke up. He was very brief and expressed the opinion of the students and teachers who were present more clearly. "The students and teachers who have come to Flins," he said, "are not trying to lead the struggle of the workers, who know very well what they have to do. They have come to offer their support and to be of service to the workers. They will only do what the workers ask them to do." These words were greeted with a storm of applause.

A representative of the local CGT union finally invited the workers to mass around the factory while a delegation went in to see the management. Some of the workers advanced toward the Mobile Guards and the CRS who were behind metal barriers in front of the factory. These latter were no doubt frightened when the first row of workers shook the barriers, and immediately they threw tear gas and grenades into the crowd. This was the beginning of the incidents.

Documents: THE VERSION OF THE CGT AND L'HUMANITE[26]

INTERVENE STRENUOUSLY AGAINST ALL ATTEMPTS TO LEAD THE WORKERS' MOVEMENT ASTRAY

Even as negotiations are carried on in the metal working industry and while preliminary consultations for the return to work continue in several other branches, provocative ventures designed to call everything into question or to push the workers into adventurous actions are beginning to take dangerously precise shape. The latest attempt of such a nature was carried out this morning at the Flins factory. After the government had ordered the occupation of the factory by the CRS and while the workers were quietly assembled, groups foreign to the working class, led by Geismar, who more and more appears as a specialist of provocation, infiltrated this assembly to incite the workers to re-occupy the factory.

These groups, trained in quasi-military fashion, who have already become notorious during operations of the same nature in

---

26. The following documents were appended to this article by its author.

the Paris region, clearly act in the service of the worst enemies of the working class. It is difficult to believe that the arrogance of the management of the metal working industry, the support it receives from the government, the police brutality against the workers and these attempts at provocation are not contrived by common consent.

CGT Union Federation of the Paris Region, June 7.

AT FLINS, THE GEISMAR GROUPS ORGANIZE
A PROVOCATION AGAINST THE RENAULT STRIKERS

Yesterday, at dawn, buses brought metal workers from neighboring villages. In front of the factory, CGT and CFDT activists had called them to a meeting at the Place de l'Etoile in Elisabethville.

[Thus, not a word on the meeting that was in fact called at Les Mureaux, 5 kilometers from Elisabethville.]

The meeting brought together almost 8000 workers. Jean Breteau, the General Secretary of the CGT Federation, proposed that a union delegation ask for the withdrawal of the police and immediate negotiation of the demands. Yves Ducos (CFDT) leaned in the same direction. Adopted.

Then a representative of the Geismar groups spoke up. Indeed, since morning, these groups (a few hundred, many of them with helmets on) had been arriving at Flins, going around or over the roadblocks that the police claim to have placed on certain roads.

Geismar's representative—who forced himself onto the platform—pretended to want to help the workers "retake" the factory. The workers never asked anything from him and protests rose from the crowd. One could hear the following: "We are here for our demands; we are well aware that the government hopes for a provocation. . . ."

Therefore, the strikers, no longer listening to Geismar's man, decided to accompany the delegation. They advanced quietly. But the first clashes occur between the group of those who call themselves students and the police. Tear gas grenades explode. . . .

L'Humanité, June 8.

[Not a word either on Geismar's intervention, while his name is mentioned three times.]

THE PEOPLE'S STUDIO

June 27 at 4:00 A.M., a large police force surrounded the Ecole des Beaux Arts, which had been occupied for 50 days. The police were acting on the orders of a judge from the "Court of State Security." The pretext was a supposed inquiry into the reconstitution of the March 22 Movement. One hundred and six students and painters were arrested and held. But it is likely that the government was mainly concerned to avenge itself on a people's studio which had produced about 600,000 copies of some 350 different posters, designed and executed in the service of the struggling workers.

The editors of the *Cahiers de Mai* publish below a document written for the *Cahiers de Mai* after a discussion in the General Assembly by the comrades who occupied the Ecole des Beaux Arts and handled the production of the people's studio.

Wednesday, May 8, the Ecole des Beaux Arts went on strike. May 13, a mass demonstration brought workers and students together in answer to the call of their unions. Political repression in the Latin quarter mobilized one million demonstrators, stretching from the Place de la Republique to the Place Denfert-Rochereau. They shouted that they would no longer tolerate the anti-popular Gaullist government, an instrument of repression by the bosses. (Nantes, Caen, Rhodiaceta, Redon.)

May 14 at 3 P.M., a provisional strike committee informed the Administration of the Ecole des Beaux Arts that the students were taking over the facilities.

May 15, the general assembly of the strikers adopted the following platform:

Why are we prolonging the struggle? Against whom are we struggling? We struggle against a class university. We want to organize the struggle against all of its aspects:
1) We criticize the social selection which takes place throughout the whole course of studies, from primary school to college, to the detriment of the children of the working class and the poor farmers. We want to struggle against the examination system, the principal means of this selection.

LA POLICE S'AFFICHE
AUX BEAUX ARTS

LES BEAUX ARTS
AFFICHENT dans la RUE

2) We criticize the content of teaching and its pedagogical forms, because everything is organized so that the products of the system fail to acquire a critical consciousness with regard to both knowledge and social and economic reality.

3) We criticize the role that the society expects intellectuals to play: watchdogs of the system of economic production, technocratic cadres; doing what is required to make everyone accept his place, especially when this "someone" is in a place of exploitation.

What do these criticisms mean for the school of painting and sculpture? Of course the commissions must define this more precisely but we can already answer for architecture:

We want to struggle against the way teaching is dominated by the profession through the Council of the Order or other corporative organisms. We are against the apprentice system as a pedagogical method, we are against the conformist ideology of the system. The teaching of architecture should not be the mere imitation of a master until the student ends up as an exact copy.

We want to struggle against the conditions of architectural production which subordinate it in practice to the interests of public and private speculation. How many architects have agreed to create big or little Sarcelles?[28] How many architects include in their cost breakdown the need of the workers on the construction site for information, hygiene, safety, and should they do so would any speculator accept their bid? And it is common knowledge that there are three deaths a day in the French construction industry.

We want to struggle against a particularly conservative, particularly irrational and unscientific course content, in which impressions and personal habits continue to prevail over objective knowledge.

The ideology of the Prize of Rome lives on!!!

In a word, we want to become conscious of the real relations between the school and the society; we want to struggle against its class character.

We must be aware that we cannot carry on this struggle alone. We must not fall into the illusion that the university community could establish in its colleges nuclei of real autonomy with

---

28. A particularly hideous public housing project that became a symbol of modernistic inhumanity.

respect to bourgeois society as a whole. The university community must struggle alongside the workers, who are the main victims of the social selection system of the schools. The struggle against the class university must be organically tied to the struggle against the capitalist system of exploitation conducted by the working class as a whole.

We must therefore commit ourselves to challenging the relationships which currently regulate the profession and teaching:

—challenge the present separation of the E.N.S.B.A. from higher education;

—refuse to implement any form of pre-selection for entry into the school;

—struggle against the present examination system;

—establish real relations of struggle with the workers.

we must have open debates on all these questions.

All teachers must express their opinion.

Forms of organization of the struggle must be developed.

Strike Committee

On May 14, several students spontaneously got together in the lithography studio and, choosing direct action, printed a first poster: FACTORY, UNIVERSITY, UNITY.

On May 16, in the course of a meeting of a reform commission constituted that same morning, some of the participants—students and painters from the outside—decided to occupy the painting studio in order to put the program of struggle defined on the 15th into practice. At the entry, they wrote:

PEOPLE'S STUDIO: YES. BOURGEOIS STUDIO: NO.

We set to work on the basis of this principle. We began to produce posters, and in the following text, distributed as a leaflet several days later on the 21st, we defined our position in relation to the debates of the reform commission at the same time.

PEOPLE'S STUDIO: YES. BOURGEOIS STUDIO: NO.

This was written on the door of the studio; if we attempt to explain, to explicate, to understand what it means, it should naturally dictate for us the basic outlines of a new activity.

This phrase means that it is not a matter of modernizing, that is to say, of improving what already is. Every improvement assumes that, at bottom, the general line remains the same, hence that it was already correct.

We are against what reigns today. What reigns today? Bourgeois art and bourgeois culture.

What is bourgeois culture? It is the instrument by which the oppressive power of the ruling class separates and isolates artists from other workers by granting them a privileged status. Privilege encloses the artist in an invisible prison. The fundamental concepts which underlie this isolating activity of the culture are:

1) the idea that art has "conquered its autonomy" (Malraux, see the speech at the time of the Olympic Games of Grenoble.)
2) the defense of the "freedom of creation." Culture makes the artist live in the illusion of freedom:
   A) He does what he wants, he believes everything to be possible, he has no obligations except to himself or to his Art.
   B) He is "creative," that is to say that he invents something unique from nothing, the value of which would presumably be permanent, above historical reality. He is not a worker dealing with historical reality. The idea of creation derealizes his work.

By granting this privileged status, culture places the artist in a position in which he can do no harm, where he functions like a safety valve in the mechanism of bourgeois society.

We are all in this situation. We are all bourgeois artists. How could it be otherwise?

This is why, when we write "people's studio," there can be no question of improvement but of a RADICAL CHANGE IN ORIENTATION.

This means that we have decided to transform what we are in society.

Let's make it clear that we are not trying to establish a better relation between artists and modern technology in order to link up more closely with other types of workers. Rather, we want to be open to the problems of other workers, that is to say, to the historical reality of the world in which we live. No professor can help us get in touch with this reality. This does not mean that there is no objective (hence transmissible) knowledge, nor that older artists, professors, cannot be very useful. But only on the condition that they themselves decide to transform what they are in the society, and participate in this labor of self-education.

With this challenge to the educational power of the bourgeoisie, the field will be open to the educational power of the people.

At that time there were ten million strikers in France. The participants of the People's Studio went out to the occupied factories, the warehouses, the construction sites, in order to learn from the striking workers how to constitute the rear of the struggle of which the workers were the vanguard. This was not a laboratory experiment. Everyone—worker or student, foreigner or French—came to participate enthusiastically in the production of posters. Workers came to propose slogans, to talk with the artists and students, to criticize or distribute posters. At the entry of the studio could be read: "To work in the people's studio is to offer concrete support to the great movement of the striking workers who occupy their factories against the anti-popular Gaullist government. In placing all his capacities in the service of the workers' struggle, each in this studio also works for himself, because he opens himself practically to the educational power of the masses." As they placed themselves concretely in the service of the people's struggle, the progressive students and artists entered the people's school and revised their point of view in linking up with the masses.

How did they work?

Projects for posters conceived by a group after a political analysis of the events of the day, or after discussions at the factory gates, were democratically proposed in the General Assembly at the end of the day.

This is how we judged:

—was the political idea correct?

—did the poster transmit this idea well?

Then the accepted projects were produced in seriograph and lithograph by teams which alternated day and night shifts.

Dozens of teams were formed to glue the posters up with the help of the Neighborhood Action Committees and the Strike Committees of the occupied factories, each relating his experiences. More and more, the various strata of the population propagated the correct ideas of the workers through these posters.

The production of posters increased. However, the main task of the People's Studio was not to flood the country from a single point, but to incite others to form new people's studios everywhere the workers were struggling, because, the political work of design and distribution must always remain linked to the struggle.

And still for us on this 22nd of June the struggle continues.
LET'S NOT BE STOPPED BY TECHNICAL DIFFICULTIES.
PUSH ONWARD!
CREATE PEOPLE'S STUDIOS EVERYWHERE!

Essay IV. Self-Management: Strategy and Goal

"Humanity will be able to live in freedom only when the last capitalist has been hanged with the entrails of the last bureaucrat."[29]

Walter Benjamin once wrote that revolution is "a tiger's leap into the past." He called on the historian of revolution to "blast open the continuum of history" and reestablish the broken links between revolutionary experiences back through the generations and the centuries.[30] The element of repetition and continuity was certainly present in the May Events. Superficially, the link was everywhere in the cobblestone barricades that recalled so many earlier Parisian insurrections. More significant was the pattern of workers' activities. Every workers' revolution in Europe since 1905 has proceeded from a general strike to the formation of "soviets," workers' councils poised to seize power from the state. In the May Events too a general strike and even a few soviets trooped back on the stage of history to perform again the play begun and interrupted so many times in this century.

Without generations of socialist propaganda by the "official" French Left, and in particular the French Communist Party, the May Events would certainly not have had such broad support from workers. And yet the communists had nothing to offer the movement in 1968.

---

29. Graffiti from the walls of Paris during the May Events. "Quel est le Sens des Elections Qui Nous Sont Imposé," published in early June by the Comité d'Action du Laboratoire de Sociologie Industrielle. "Nous Continuous la Lutte," May 28, Comité d'Action Ouviers-Etudiants.

30. Walter Benjamin, *Illuminations* (New York: Schocken, 1968), 261–262.

The most important difference between the communists and the new opposition movements concerned the attitude toward the state. By May 1968 the French Communist Party was fully committed to an electoral strategy. Its goal was to put together an "anti-monopoly alliance" capable of winning an electoral majority and creating "an advanced democracy as a step toward socialism." But at this time the French communists were among the most loyal supporters of the Soviet Union outside Russia. Their intended allies, moderate socialist parties representing employees, small businessmen, and farmers, were unalterably opposed to the Russian model of socialism. The Party denied dictatorial intentions and insisted that it was committed to democracy. Yet it never criticized the absence of this desirable system in the Soviet Union, a lapse that left its sincerity open to question.

Furthermore, communist strategy identified socialism with a program of extensive nationalizations that, the students charged, would leave the bureaucratic apparatus of the state and the corporations intact and concentrate ever more power at the top. Meanwhile, moderate socialists saw their role as restraining such impulses toward centralization by maintaining the separation of the economy and the state that has always been the foundation of the liberal conception of freedom. The resulting alliance appeared to be self-canceling.

The problem was in fact insoluble as it was posed by these parties. The old freedoms are withering in any case through the growing identification of giant corporations and the state, the organized planning of the economy by monopolies and oligopolies, the increasing bureaucratization of major social institutions, and the ever more effective manipulation of voters by the mass media. The communist strategy would seem to change only the men at the top, but not the oppressive structure. Nationalization of the economy would simply complete the technocratic project of monopoly capitalism itself, whatever its social content.

The mainstream of the student movement rejected the entire political strategy of these left parties. The error, they argued, lay in situating the struggle on the electoral plane, taking the state as the object and not the enemy in the struggle. Instead, the students demanded an end to the technocratic division of labor as the basis for a radically new model of socialist society.

Furthermore, the revolutionaries argued, given the organization of modern capitalism, given its institutionalized power in every sphere of daily life, given its control of mass culture, an electoral victory of the Left would be, if not impossible, at the very least a feeble substitute for a real revolution attacking the sources of social reproduction. As one leaflet notes,

> In the present situation . . . the system's integrative models of mass consumption and the search for social advancement . . . actually represent the modern form of oppression, which is no longer materialized exclusively in the State. The instrument of capitalist power thus no longer resides so much in this latter [the state] as in the submission of workers to models of consumer society and to all the differentiated forms of authority that insure its functioning.

This analysis has not been refuted by the later history of French socialism in power.

It was for such reasons that the activists of May demanded a socialism arising from a mass revolutionary movement, one that would not simply change the men at the top of the hierarchy but would shatter that hierarchy and replace it with democratic self-management. Socialism was to emerge not from an electoral victory, but through the transformation of the general strike into an "active strike" in which the workers would set their factories back into motion on their own account. (Something like this actually occurred in a number of localities.)[31] Then, with the economy turning again, but for the workers and not for their former bosses, the state would quickly succumb. A parallel power would arise in each town and village as workers coordinated their efforts with each other and the farmers. Socialism would be initiated from below and not handed down from above in nationalizations.

Self-management, one of the goals of this socialist revolution, would also serve as a strategy in the struggle against capitalism. This strategy had a triple edge. First, it would end the lethargy and atomization of the general strike, facilitate the independent organization of the workers as a powerful political force, and make it very difficult for the government to mobilize against the secession of whole industries and regions. Second, as a consequence, it would ensure a passage from capitalism to socialism in a way that would limit the power of the state after the revolution, safeguarding the new society from Stalinism. Third, the active strike was supposed to alter the ideological balance of power between capital and labor by showing the obsolescence of

---

31. Yannick Guin, *La Commune de Nantes* (Paris: Maspero, 1969).

capitalist management. If workers did not need the capitalists to run the economy, the entire population would be encouraged to follow them. As one leaflet put it, "Demonstrate that workers' management in the factories is the power to do better for everyone what the capitalists did scandalously for a few."

In France industrial democracy has an anarchist ring. In fact, the revival of the black flag during May was an astonishing reminder of a whole French anarchist tradition long thought to be dead outside a few musty sects. Everyone was aware of this historical reference, and yet the concept of self-management was not the product of the surviving anarchist sects but of the actual struggle pursued to its logical conclusion.

In this respect the May Events are better compared with the last great wave of European revolutions that followed World War I, in which millions of workers in many nations more or less spontaneously formed workers' councils to bring industrialism under the direct control of the immediate producers. Everywhere but in Russia these revolutions were defeated, and we know the fate of workers' councils in the Soviet Union. What we cannot say for sure is that they would have failed so completely in richer countries such as Germany, which also had revolutions in this period and might have offered the council communist program a more suitable terrain than Russia. Soon Stalinism was to bury the issue in any case.

But the May Events revived it under the name of self-management. This movement could be seen as a radical return to the idea of *social* revolution, a revolution that displaces the state from the center of the stage to allow initiative from below to substitute itself for political domination from a fixed center. Black flags flew alongside red ones in France during May, but the synthesis of the two was widely understood as a revival of the submerged libertarian trend in Marxism itself, in opposition to all established models of socialism.

But was the general strike of May and June truly revolutionary? Was it an economic or a political movement, a movement for wage increases or for socialism? Posed in this form the question is unanswerable. The mass strike, considered as a recurring pattern of working class resistance, is always both economic and political, and so were the Events.[32]

---

32. Rosa Luxemburg, "The Mass Strike, the Political Party and the Trade Unions," in *Rosa Luxemburg Speaks*, M.-A. Waters, ed. (New York: Pathfinder, 1970), p. 186.

Yet the penultimate moment of the May Events is most significai.
the moment in which the workers and students demanded the resignation of a government that could no longer even control the state bureaucracy, much less run the country. In this moment of hesitation at the end
of May the nation hung in suspense while the workers and the government weighed their chances. In this moment the movement became
something more than a mere summation of particular struggles for
immediate interests. Massive disobedience to authority in every sphere,
whatever its immediate occasion, set off a chain reaction in the crucible
of which a political will was formed.

To call the May Events a "revolution," it is not necessary to show
that the government could have been overthrown by an insurrection at
this point. The defining characteristic of a revolution is not that it is
stronger than the state, but that it abruptly calls the existing society into
question in the minds of millions and effectively presses them into
action. A revolution is an attempt by these millions to influence the
resolution of a profound social crisis by violent or illegal means, reestablishing the community on new bases. This is precisely what happened during May. Social forms melted down into the individuals
whose cooperation within their framework had made possible the old
society. This was what an earlier French revolutionary, Saint-Just, called
"the public moment," the moment in which the social contract is re-
viewed and reconstituted in action.[33]

The Texts

"The Revolutionary Action Committee of the Sorbonne." These leaflets issued during the May Events were later collected by their authors
in a mimeographed brochure accompanied by informative commen-
taries on the uses to which they were put, the quantity circulated, and
the response of the recipients. The brochure shows the development of
the key strategic idea of the active strike. We present a selection of these
leaflets.

"The University as a Red Base." This and the next two articles
describe the movement in the city of Nantes, where it reached its ap-
ogee. This first article concerns the development of the student movement in that city. It was published in *Les Cahiers de Mai,* June 15, 1968.

"Nantes: A Whole Town Discovers the Power of the People." The factory occupation movement began at Sud-Aviation in

---

33. Louis Antoine de Saint-Just, *L'Esprit de la Révolution.* (Paris: UGE, 1963), p. 20.

Nantes. This article, by a group of students sent out from Paris, describes the situation in the town as workers gradually seized control. The article first appeared in *Action,* June 10, 1968, and was reprinted in *Les Cahiers de Mai,* June 15, 1968.

"From Roadblocks to Self-Defense." This article is a continuation of the preceding one. It describes the formation of an incipient revolutionary "government" on the basis of the regional strike committees in Nantes. This article was originally published in *Action,* June 11, 1968, and reprinted in *Les Cahiers de Mai,* June 15, 1968.

THE REVOLUTIONARY ACTION COMMITTEE
OF THE SORBONNE

BY WAY OF AN INTRODUCTION[34]

This brochure . . . presents as an example the activities of two Action Committees: the Revolutionary Action Committee of the Sorbonne (CARS) and the Italian Worker-Student Action Committee of the Sorbonne. It was edited by the comrades of these two committees, or rather by those who remained after the numerous repressions of the government.

We have collected what seemed to us the most important texts among all those printed by the CARS during the occupation of the Sorbonne.

We hope the reader will plunge back into the spirit of May to fully understand certain texts that may appear outdated today. . . .

How were these two committees constituted? Essentially by the will to struggle of numerous students, workers, unemployed comrades and others . . . who for the most part did not know each other before what was called the occupation of the Sorbonne—which we prefer to call its temporary liberation.

Some were already politicized but the majority got their revolutionary experience in the course of the days and nights of action, discussions, and contacts during May.

---

34. These introductory remarks were written by the authors of the leaflets reproduced in this document.

WHAT WAS THE MINIMUM POLITICAL PLATFORM TACITLY ACCEPTED BY ALL? ESSENTIALLY:

1) The transcendence of political and union organizations, whether they be petty bourgeois or extreme Left.
2) The transcendence of the narrow theoretical structures of these organizations.
3) The deeply felt sentiment we all shared, based either on science or intuition, that the Sorbonne could not and should not be anything more than a temporary base for revolutionary action.
4) The conviction that our task was to facilitate the working class struggle and to enable it to overflow a suffocating reformist framework.
5) The refusal to be constructive or "realistic" about the "natural economic laws," those traps set by the government into which many students fell, not to speak of the union organizations (but for them it is an old tradition).
6) The rejection of bourgeois legality in favor of a scientific analysis of the balance of forces.
7) Above all, the deep conviction that the exploitation of man by man must disappear.

Otherwise, to avoid ideological quarrels, we deliberately ignored each other's political labels or lack of labels. This was how we were able to struggle side by side in the framework of political discussions over definite political ideas without ending up in provincial quarrels but on the contrary in revolutionary political action. Discussion became operational and the practice-theory-practice dialectic could finally be applied without prejudice. Far from slowing things down, the relative diversity of tendencies became a dynamic factor. . . .

Let us turn now to the problem of distribution and propaganda. At first this job was carried out by volunteer distributors but the Italian Action Committee soon took charge, dividing up into night teams and limiting its activity to the factories. And we must emphasize the enormous labor of politicization our Italian comrades accomplished with the help of the comrades of the CARS.

A leaflet is not an end in itself: it is a means to achieve certain ends. Depending on the nature of the texts and the goal, the quality of the distribution and propaganda is often more important than the text itself.

This is why we ask the reader to dive back into the atmosphere of May and to imagine the discussions, the conflicts, and even brawls we sometimes had with the workers we had gone to see, which were necessary for everyone to gradually achieve a mutual respect. This was the price we had to pay to contribute to the level of political struggle of all the exploited and prepare ever more violent and ever more fruitful confrontations for tomorrow.

We conclude with these two phrases, drawn from two leaflets in this brochure:

"This is only a beginning, we are continuing the struggle."

"Power is there to take."

It is for all revolutionaries to take it and to destroy it immediately. Because, we do not want a state capitalism and a bureaucratic and criminal red bourgeoisie. The revolution of 1917 has taught us how a few "professional revolutionaries" can completely pervert a soviet revolution in a few months time: we will try to keep this in mind.

[leaflet #1]

STUDENT WORKER ACTION COMMITTEE—MAY 17

Comrade workers,

After a week of cobblestones, riot police and combat gas, the students of Paris have occupied the Sorbonne.

It has become the autonomous and popular university of Paris. This means that:

1) We are at home there, we have taken power there. We no longer accept orders imposed from above.
2) We refuse the education that was forced upon us, because we refuse to become your future exploiting bosses.
3) From now on, the Sorbonne also belongs to workers: together we will make the decisions regarding our activities.
4) We desire the presence of workers, and if they request it, we will organize classes on problems that interest them, and especially secondary education in the factories at night.
5) Between your problems and ours there are certain similarities:
    employment and job opportunities
    standards and work pace
    union freedoms
    self-management
6) The workers of Nantes show the way. They occupy the factory and weld the bureaucrats' door shut to block the way to com-

promises. Everywhere the rule is the same: let's not slavishly execute the orders of a minority which only wants to manage us the better to exploit us.

Comrade workers, join us at the university!

Welcome the students in your companies as you are welcomed at the Sorbonne.

Let us unite in the: Worker-student action committees

(inter-union)

100 meetings at 6:00, Friday May 17 in Paris and suburbs

[leaflet #2]

This leaflet, written by the Action Committee of the Condorcet High School was chosen as an example from among the innumerable leaflets of this kind which were communicated to us and which we published and often distributed. (The high school action committees (CAL) were often semi-clandestine groups and we had a much greater freedom of action than did some of our high school comrades.) This activity in the high schools was one of our basic objectives because we believe that the more politicization occurs in the early "grades," the lower the age of politicization, the better chance we will have of seeing new and explosive theories elaborated. We deliberately risk being treated as moderates in two or three years but this will be a magnificent consecration for us.

Disrespect and operational revolutionary creativity must break out at all levels, and sharp discussions as well as reprisals will not be lacking in the years to come. But the search for pre-revolutionary conditions cannot take place in tranquility. And we think that an essential strategy of the movement should be to provoke a chain reaction reaching younger and younger comrades, because bourgeois "EDUCATION" imposes servitudes on the human being from his earliest years.[35]

"CONDORCET" HIGH SCHOOL IS OCCUPIED—MAY 20

Today, May 20. After a week of struggle, the High School Action Committee decided on the autonomy of "Condorcet" High School.

---

35. This commentary, like similar italicized texts at the beginning of the leaflets in this document, was written by the authors of the leaflets.

It declares its solidarity with the struggle of the students and workers.

It requests all students to come to "Condorcet" to debate the various problems which concern them.

THE HIGH SCHOOL WILL BE OCCUPIED DAY AND NIGHT, FOR AN UNLIMITED PERIOD.

The Condorcet High School C.A.L.

[leaflet #3]

THE MOVEMENT RECALLS THAT

1) The campus occupations are only a partial aspect of its action.
2) The occupation and the tasks performed during it should serve the general struggle against the capitalist system.

The occupation responds to the following political objectives:

1) To neutralize university operations momentarily in order to neutralize capitalist academic legality.
2) To organize the students for a radical contestation of the society and the University.
3) To establish a base for the movement.

THE CAMPUS BEING A PLACE FOR:
—organizing the movement into action committees,
—discussion within the movement and with the outside world,
—for the preparation of projected actions.

In this way, the campus occupations take on a new dimension during the development of the workers' movement, and are themselves a test of strength which can lead to several outcomes:

—Either the collapse of the movement and the re-opening of the campuses, reformed or not,

—Or the pure and simple overthrow of the regime.

The campus occupations must therefore be extended, prolonged, and organized in connection with the development of the workers' movement.

Considering that the political goal is really the overthrow of the regime by the workers and that the occupations should be organized in this political framework,

—that education will not respond to the people's needs until they have actually destroyed the capitalist state.

—that the reconstruction of the University cannot be envisaged outside this framework, and should, therefore, be the creation not only of those people who now work there but of all the workers.

—[the movement] will oppose reform of the capitalist University, and will consequently boycott the formation of paritary commissions.

Denounces generally:

—attempts orchestrated by certain professors to sidetrack the movement by trapping it in the narrow framework of university reformism, as well as the student folklore into which the occupations risk falling.

Recalls that the essential task of the students is to join up with the fight of the working class against the regime.

Worker-Student Action Committee

[leaflet #4]

This leaflet was written by the Italian Worker-Student Action Committee of the Sorbonne after a sharp discussion between our two committees which lasted a whole night long. This too is a combat leaflet and it contributed to organizing the transcendence of struggle on the barricades, which was falling into student folklore. On the other hand it was a very good basis of discussion in the factories where it was distributed. The Action Committee appeared as the prolongation of the political revelation of the night of Friday the tenth. It appeared as a way of preventing the government from digesting the barricades by transforming them into repetitive phenomena and turning the cobblestone into a consumer product. (50,000 copies)

COMRADES—MAY 31

The absence of a revolutionary party requires the formation of a revolutionary vanguard.

The action committees are the only groups corresponding to such a necessity. They must not be the fruit of negotiations over formulas supported by different political groups, parties or unions.

The basic role of the action committees is THE POLITICIZATION OF THE WORKING CLASS STRUGGLE. We must achieve the transcendence of traditional political and union structures with their help.

It is thus necessary to fight every attempt at reformist co-optation directed from the bureaucratic summits of the PCF and CGT. The principal goal must be to clear the way as much as possible towards SOCIAL-IST CONSCIOUSNESS.

The action committees should oppose their own revolutionary legality to the Gaullist government and the purely parliamentary and legal action of the Left.

Only the action committees, expressing their full revolutionary creativity, can develop a unified political line. They are *political barricades,* capable of directing the revolutionary struggle, that is to say:

—To support the strike until *the coming of an authentic workers' power.*

—To support or direct all other forms of struggle, such as for example, the fee strike in public services. This enables the prolonged or unlimited occupation of the factories to take place without the strikers bearing the whole burden; and, on the other hand, makes it possible to abolish the monopoly of the capitalist state over its essential mechanism of accumulation and distribution.

It is also a specific duty of the action committees to create adequate forms of self-defense:

—Against police violence,

—Against the civic committees, that is to say, against the bourgeoisie which organizes itself in a *fascist manner* to defend its "*Capitalist Freedom.*"

Historical experience has taught us that attack is the workers' movement's only defense.

The present situation demands an emphasis on the deep link between the revolutionary struggle in France and anti-imperialist struggles at the world level. Peace is not in the "tranquillity" of acquired positions, but in continuous war against the imperialist cancer.

Worker-Student Action Committee

[leaflet #5]

This text is one of the all too rare attempts to enlarge the bearing of the situation in the month of May. Tactically, it concerned the creation of circuits of direct distribution to permit the strike to hold out. Strategically, the goal was to prime the awakening of political consciousness among farmers, who are both very tough and very courageous in their demands but who often also feel a sickly and absurd fear of the "reds."

The comrades who distributed these leaflets, in Brittany for the most part, denounced an economic system which forced farmers to dump their potatoes in the streets while the strikers had a terrible time getting food. They often succeeded in making the farmers clearly aware of the absurd economic contradictions of a distribution system based on price fixing by exploitative monopolies.

This awakening of consciousness made it possible, in particular, to set up shipments of potatoes with the help of the SNCF (National Railroad Company), operating on this occasion in an active strike. But going still further, many farmer comrades expressed the wish to remain in contact with the propagandists of the movement and to connect their struggle with that of the working class and the students. Note in this regard that we have much to learn from the increasingly frequent experiments in Italy, particularly in the northern provinces.

COMRADE FARMERS

The people of Paris and of France are united in the struggle against a cruel and stupid government so that the entire labor force may really participate in the economic, social and political life of the country.

Farmers: there is no agricultural policy

The Common Market makes its decisions without consulting you

Appropriations are insufficient

Who guarantees price stability for your products?

For a quick and effective solution
EVERYONE UNITED IN ACTION

The ten million strikers committed to struggling all the way ask the farmers to support them.

THE STRIKERS AND THEIR FAMILIES MUST BE GIVEN FOOD.

HOW?
By placing the products of your work in the cooperatives

WE WILL DISTRIBUTE THEM?

YOU TOO SHOULD ORGANIZE YOURSELVES IN ACTION COMMITTEES

ALL TOGETHER IN A SINGLE FORCE

WE WILL WIN!
Farmer-Worker-Student Action Committee

[leaflet #6]

We wrote this text at the request of comrades in the army who handled its distribution in their barracks. The objective was twofold:

1. *Strategic: it always seemed obvious to us that revolution is impossible unless deep tensions appear in the army.*
2. *Political: given its class interests and the way it is recruited, the army was directly concerned by the development of the situation.*
   (20,000 copies)

COMRADE SOLDIERS—MAY 31

In the wake of strikes unleashed by all the workers of FRANCE, the government has organized a savage police repression against the struggling students and workers.

The government no longer holds the factories, nor the universities, nor the public institutions.

Only force remains, that is to say, the CRS and the career army, with which to crush the people in struggle.

Today it is preparing to give you the order to shoot at the French people, on your relatives and your friends.

You cannot allow yourselves to be the instruments of a massacre ordered by a backward looking government which no longer represents the popular will.

Comrade soldiers, struggle with us in order to return as soon as possible to civilian life, participate with us in the renewal of the society.
Worker-Student Action Committee

[leaflet #7]

This is a combat leaflet written by the Revolutionary Action Committee of the Sorbonne and printed in more than 150,000 copies.

A BAS

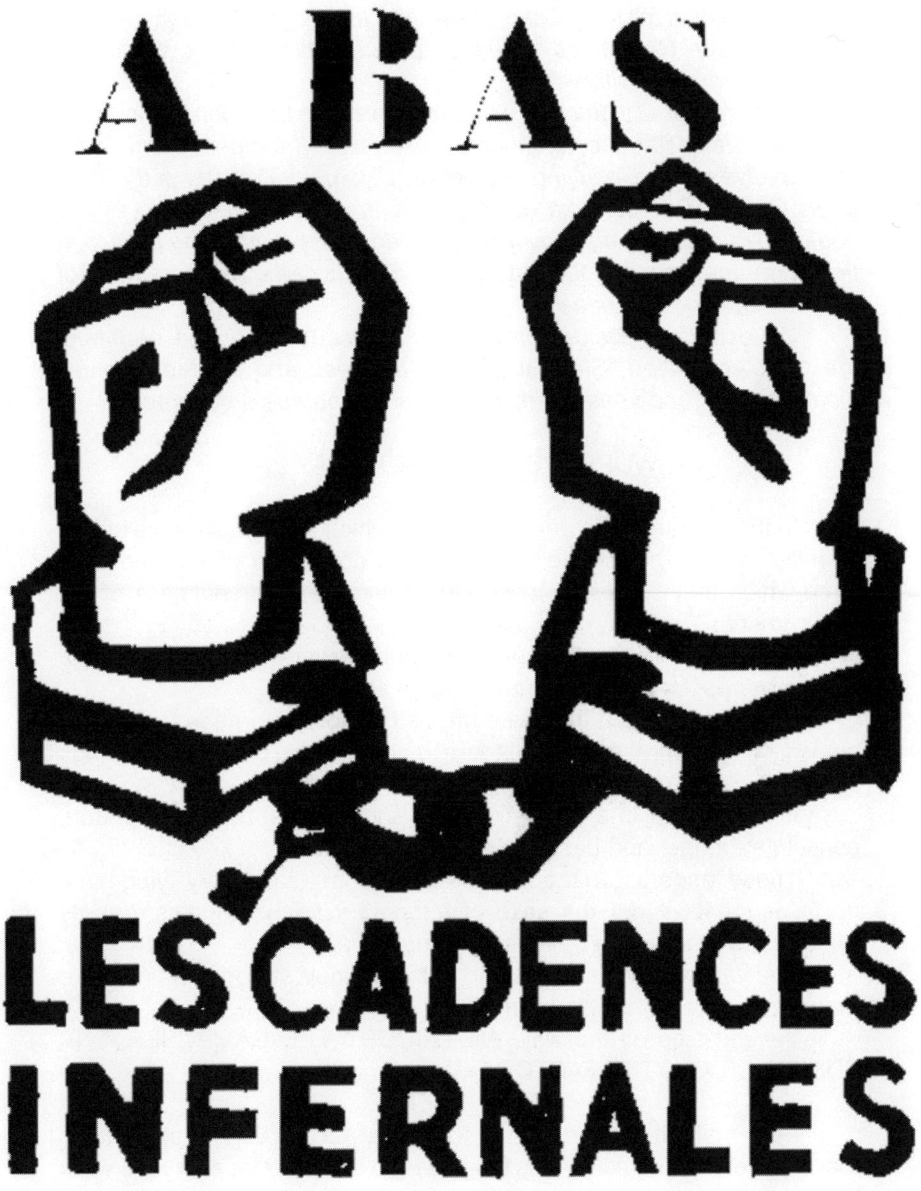

LES CADENCES INFERNALES

Different versions were produced as the situation developed. Distribution was handled for the most part by night teams of the Italian Worker-Student Action Committee of the Sorbonne, which always worked in close collaboration with us.

The main goal in this text was to organize the transcendence of the CGT on its left without cutting ourselves off from the masses and opening ourselves to the insulting attacks of "L'Humanité" or the petty bourgeois Séguy. This schema corresponds to a tactic which the CARS constantly applied: to fight over political ideas to promote the politicization of the masses, and thus to limit the actions of the top leadership of the PCF as much as possible.

We especially avoided direct attacks because when the leaders of the CGT are called "Stalinist creeps" the rank and file feels deeply insulted and it becomes nearly impossible to pursue a dialogue.

WORKERS-STUDENTS—MAY 20

In the course of the demonstrations which have shaken the sterile "Gaullist order," the people have become conscious of the immense force which they represent while measuring the real weakness of the government.

In 10 years of Gaullist rule, they have experienced the complete ineffectiveness of the traditional forms of struggle.

Management and the State are astounded. A terrified Capitalism pleads for the "representative leaders" of the working class to take things in hand.

It knows that in a period of deep social crisis, reformist leaders constitute the last and best rampart of the regime.

These leaders turn the workers away from total victory, tying them up in negotiations for the sake of temporary financial gains, quickly wiped out by the rise in the cost of living.

The workers and students do not want their struggle to finish like the movements of 1936 and 1945.

We must go all the way. WE OCCUPY THE CAMPUSES, THE BUREAUCRACY, THE FACTORIES . . .
STAY THERE

Let's make them run by and for ourselves, showing that workers' management in the factories is the power to do better for everyone what the capitalists did scandalously for a few.

Do not let bourgeois or social-democratic politicians negotiate the return to order in exchange for a ministry.

Force de Gaulle's departure and the creation of a workers' government. The government we want must institute direct democracy within a socialism based on the proposals of rank and file committees.

These committees must assure its effective realization. Do Not Fall into the Trap of Sterile Discussions.

Power is There to Take.

TAKE IT

Worker-Student Action Committee

[leaflet #8]

This text was written by the CARS at a time when the need was felt for an intermediate type of leaflet, between the fighting leaflet, which no longer sufficed, and the pamphlet, which nobody read. At that time there was a general strike and the problem of political power was posed.

It was distributed essentially in the factories. The tactic was as follows. We began by interesting the workers in the problem of self-management and mass political power with:

"Workers-Students" or "The Struggle Continues."

Then we distributed some "We Are Continuing the Struggle" in sufficiently small numbers to create groups. In each group a worker comrade played the role of discussion leader. Politics ceased to be a disgusting thing, a pile of corrupt and careerist politicians and became everyone's right to play a role in social life. In each group the workers ceased thinking of the stopped machines as something which was going to start up again after trivial and temporary wage increases. Operated by and for the worker, the machine would make it possible to force the capitalists back to their final bastion.

This was truly a fascinating experience and in some small and middle sized factories experiments in self-management were tried for several weeks.

This was already quite good and will make it possible in the next spontaneous strikes to reach this stage much more quickly and to force the CGT to run once again in the race to catch up with the rank and file.

But a day will come when it will no longer be able to catch up . . . (30,000 copies)

WE ARE CONTINUING THE STRUGGLE—MAY 28

Our goal is obviously not to destroy the present structures without proposing something new, contrary to the insinuations of Gaullist slander.

The absence of a leader at the head of our movement today corresponds to its very nature. It is not a matter of knowing who will be at the head of all, but how all will form a single head. More precisely, there can be no question of the appropriation of the movement by some political or union organization that was already in place before the movement was formed.

The unity of this movement must not and cannot come from the premature presence of a celebrity at its head but from the unity of aspirations of the workers, farmers and students. These aspirations can take on a concrete form in grass roots committees through small group discussions. These committees will then gradually efface the inevitable differences amongst themselves that will have appeared. UNITY MUST COME FROM THE GRASS ROOTS AND NOT FROM A PREMATURE LEADER WHO CANNOT NOW TAKE INTO ACCOUNT THE ASPIRATIONS OF ALL THE WORKERS.[36]

But this work of unification will encounter the worst external difficulties and will not be accomplished without effective mastery of the street which is the place of political contestation and discussion. Pompidou understood this well when he pretended to grant (!) us everything except the street.

However, difficulties can also come from within. Indeed, we must watch out for a thoughtless anti-Gaullism which could encourage some of us to believe that the problem will be solved automatically by the departure of de Gaulle and his government.

The movement cannot endorse an operation of the "popular front" type or a transitional government. The material concessions that we could obtain would in no way change the scandalous character of the present society. Besides, they would be quickly absorbed by a rise in the cost of living organized by the bosses.

This is why the ultimate weapon of the workers struggling for revolution is DIRECT MANAGEMENT of their means of coordination and production.

Another step must be taken!!!

Comrades, the occupation of the factories must now signify that you are capable of making them function without the bourgeois frame-

---

36. The "premature leader" in question is no doubt Mendès-France or Mitterand.

work which exploited you. The revolutionary movement must now be allowed to live, to develop itself, to organize production under your control. You thereby deprive capitalism of its instruments of oppression. Assure production, distribution: the entire working class must prove that a workers' power in possession of its own means of production can establish a real socialist economy.

The goal of SELF-MANAGEMENT AS AN ECONOMIC AND SOCIAL SYSTEM is to fully achieve free participation in production and consumption through individual and collective responsibility. It is therefore a system created above all for humanity, to serve and not to oppress.

Practically, self-management consists in the worker comrades operating their factories by and for themselves and, consequently, the elimination of the hierarchy of salaries as well as the notions of wage earner and boss. They should set up the workers' councils, elected by themselves to carry out the decisions of the whole.

These councils must be in close relation with the councils of other enterprises on the regional, national and international plane.

The members of these workers' councils are elected for a specified term and their tasks are rotated. It is necessary in practice to avoid recreating a bureaucracy which would tend to set up a leadership and an oppressive power.

DEMONSTRATE THAT WORKERS' MANAGEMENT OF THE FIRM IS THE POWER TO DO BETTER FOR EVERYONE WHAT THE CAPITALISTS DID SCANDALOUSLY FOR A FEW.

Follow our comrades at the CSF who have shown the way for several days now.

We must also create new structures of exchange to enable us to do without middlemen who take a totally unjustified profit to the detriment of the worker and consumer (wholesalers, bankers, stock brokers, etc. . . .)

Comrades, we must go all the way:

WE OCCUPY THE CAMPUSES, THE BUREAUCRACY, THE FACTORIES.

STAY THERE AND MAKE THEM FUNCTION FOR OURSELVES AS SOON AS POSSIBLE BECAUSE CAPITALISM IS TRYING TO STARVE US OUT.

SHOW THAT WE ARE RESPONSIBLE FOR THE GIGANTIC MOVEMENT WE HAVE JUST CREATED.

DO NOT FALL INTO THE TRAP OF STERILE DISCUSSIONS.

LET'S NOT BE IMPRESSED BY THE SLANDERS AND THREATS OF AN OLD MAN WHO PRETENDS TO REPRESENT FRANCE WITHOUT TAKING ITS INHABITANTS INTO ACCOUNT.

CAPITALISM IS FRIGHTENED AND SHOWS ITS TRUE ASPECT: FASCISM. BUT POWER IS THERE FOR THE TAKING.

LET'S TAKE IT

Worker-Student Action Committee

[leaflet #9]

This leaflet was written by the Revolutionary Action Committee of the Sorbonne and distributed for the most part in the factories. In it will be found ideas which we continually defended:

—the indispensable nature of circuits of direct distribution in order to be able to continue the strike and to prevent the capitalists from starving it out.

—the idea that the factory occupations can only be a first step, after which three possibilities emerge:

a) *work starts up again with "victories" that fool no one.*
b) *the above-mentioned factories get burned down.*
c) *they are made to function by an active strike, by and for the strikers. This has the dual advantage of preparing the socialist society of tomorrow and costing capitalism infinitely more.*

(20,000 copies)

THIS IS ONLY A BEGINNING—WE ARE CONTINUING THE STRUGGLE—JUNE 1

Everyone who is really committed to the pursuit of the struggle begun by the students must join together to form a real revolutionary unity with the goal of overthrowing the present regime, and destroying the present system to construct a society in which all forms of oppression will be eliminated.

WORKERS CONTINUE TO OCCUPY YOUR WORKPLACE

The struggle is wherever you are. Lock up your management peacefully: that many fewer enemies to oppose you on the outside, and if possible set your workplace going again for yourselves, linking up with the movement so as to aid it according to your means.

LONG LIVE DIRECT MANAGEMENT, REVOLUTIONARY ARM OF THE FIGHTING WORKERS.

WAR MUST NOW BE DECLARED ON THE INSTITUTIONS.

NOW IS THE TIME TO REJECT EVERY PARLIAMENTARY AND UNION MANEUVER DESIGNED TO PERVERT THE STRUGGLE IN WHICH WE ARE ENGAGED.

Worker-Student Action Committee

[leaflet #10]

This is a combat leaflet. It was printed up several times in more than 100,000 copies, with slight modifications made in the text with each printing. In writing it we attempted to show people a way out of a strike which continued to rot, in spite of the magnificent courage of the worker comrades. The goal was to make it possible to get beyond the stage of union demands in reality, no longer just in wishes. Hence we distributed these leaflets in all the factories in the Paris region and at Sud-Aviation in Toulouse. It should be noted that this leaflet was very well received and that we could then distribute "We Are Continuing the Struggle."

We thus provided a minimum theoretical base for small group discussion. The work was particularly fruitful at Thomson, CSF-Paris-Talbot, etc.

THE STRUGGLE CONTINUES—JUNE 5

The government has responded to all our essential demands by:

—intimidation;

—wage raises which will be eaten up in six months by RISING PRICES.

On the other hand, it gives no response concerning:

—WORKERS' POWER IN THE FACTORIES;

—THE RESPONSIBILITY of workers for the MANAGEMENT of the company;

—THE UNITY reflected by the common aspirations of workers and students.

COMRADES, the occupation of the factories and the campuses should signify that we are capable of supervising their operation without the bourgeois framework which exploited us.

SHOW THAT WORKERS' MANAGEMENT IN THE FACTORIES IS THE POWER TO DO BETTER FOR EVERYONE WHAT THE CAPITALISTS DID SCANDALOUSLY FOR A FEW.
COMRADES,
CAPITALISM IS TRYING TO TAKE BACK WHAT IS OURS:
—THE FACTORIES AND THE CAMPUSES.
Worker-Student Action Committee

THE UNIVERSITY AS A RED BASE

The students of Nantes played the same role in their city as the Nanterre *"enragés"* played in the later paralysis of the country as a whole. Against the background of the farm crisis, they were the catalysts of the general movement of contestation.

As early as the first quarter, a few trouble-makers posed the problem of sexual segregation in the dormitories. Having obtained the repeal of the house rules (as at Nanterre a little later), the students felt the need to go beyond the framework of their own problems by supporting the struggle of the employees in the dorms and the cafeterias; it was largely because of the students that 75 percent of the personnel were unionized at the end of December.

At the beginning of the second quarter, the same activists picketed the cafeteria "to protest against working conditions and wages"; they took over the leadership of UNEF and the MNEF (January 20th) not to strengthen those institutions but to use the material means they had at their disposal.

February 14 was a key date, a national day of protest by dorm residents; the demonstration and the invasion of the Chancellor's office ended with a treacherous attack by the police. There were numerous wounded and arrests.

The next day the whole city was scandalized by the brutality of the CRS. Here, as at Nanterre, every advance of the repression brought with it a widening of the struggle. A university strike began which lasted several days; the students held discussions with their professors and distributed leaflets in the factories. Note that during this period the UEC (Union of Communist Students, affiliated with the Communist Party) had the same treacherous policy as at Nanterre, avoiding these early acts of contestation and even denouncing "anarchist provocateurs" the day after the police beatings!

After that until Easter there was only a small demonstration on March 15.

But the Paris events had repercussions in Nantes from the beginning of May. On May 7 students and professors began a strike in connection with the national movement. On May 8 they participated out of solidarity in the worker and farmer demonstrations. It should be said that contact with the workers' unions, which was rather cold at first, improved in and through the common struggle.

The FO, the CFDT and the CGT (not without reservations) later agreed to collaborate, culminating in student participation in the Central Strike Committee from May 30 on. Before this, when Sud-Aviation started a wildcat strike on May 14, the students rushed in with moral and material support (money, blankets taken from the dorms). They were everywhere, reinforcing the picket lines; they defended the road blocks alongside the truckers (see the article "Toward Self-Defense").

Thanks to the dynamism of their struggle the students rallied new troops: the conservative colleges (law, pharmacy, medicine), disgusted by the violence of the cops, rushed headlong into the fight. In the Law School, they refused to take the exams and proclaimed their autonomy. The high school students also followed after May 11, when they invaded the Nantes railway station together with the college students. They formed High School Action Committees and from then on participated in all the activities.

The legitimacy and efficacy of the more radical forms of action [were] mainly imposed by the students—and all the other young people with them. Sanctions were imposed by the chancellor's office after the incidents of February l4; the 10,000 franc scholarship was canceled. Petitions and protests were unsuccessful. But when, after the unitary demonstration of May 13, students and workers fought at the Prefecture, they obtained satisfaction on those two points by showing their force and resolution. Even the most militant did not preach violence for its own sake; yet like the farmers, they observed that given the authoritarian nature of the present regime the only way to be heard is through violence in the streets.

On the other hand, the Faculty of Letters has had the interesting idea of organizing discussions on parochial schools for the last ten days. Fifty percent of the pre-baccalaureate students are in Catholic education.[37] Thanks to the general climate of cultural revolution this was the first time that the problem had been squarely faced by teachers from the public and private sector. Thus a decisive step was taken towards the unification of education right in the middle of Chouan country.[38]

Sectarian divisions between leftist students have become secondary thanks to the struggle. Farmers and workers visited the university out of curiosity, but this can be the start of a true opening of the universities to the people. Right now the students are struggling on two fronts:

—Within, they are trying to prevent reformist co-optation. Certain students do not understand the depth of the present crisis: the absurdity of exams, the anti-democratic character of admissions policy, the isolation of studies from the problems of real life. Instead of looking for solutions together with the workers and farmers, they just seek piecemeal reform, or they accept Gaullist objectives inscribed in the Fifth Plan.

—On the outside, they participate actively in the strike and are already thinking about the organization of a People's University for the future. Banners in all their demonstrations demand the admission of all young workers to the inexpensive student cafeteria. The farmers' unions have been contacted to coordinate with the campuses the professional education required for the development of proletarianized agricultural workers.

Six months ago everybody said: "You students criticize everything, you want to destroy everything, but you don't know what to put in its place. There will be chaos!"

Today, in the course of the struggle, day care centers have been improvised on all the campuses and, more generally, new forms of organization have emerged.

This confidence in the creativity of the movement is the greatest contribution of student agitation.

---

37. The French baccalaureate is equivalent to an American high school diploma.

38. The Chouan participated in a counterrevolutionary movement during the French Revolution of 1789. This region of France was long noted for its Catholic and reactionary politics.

NANTES: A WHOLE TOWN DISCOVERS THE POWER OF THE PEOPLE

(This is the collective account of a trip to Nantes made by three comrades from Nanterre University: Bernard Conein, Bernard Granotier and Henri Fournie.)[39]

WORKING CLASS COMBATIVITY IN THE OCCUPIED FACTORIES

We chose two companies as tests of working class combativity: Sud-Aviation Bouguenais and A.C.B. (ship building). Numerous discussions with worker unionists also enabled us to get an idea of the degree of class consciousness among the workers of Nantes; in particular, we attended meetings of the railroad workers' inter-union Strike Committee.

Contact with the Sud-Aviation Bouguenais factory seemed especially important to us since this was the first company occupied by its workers, and played the role of "detonator" in unleashing the general strike.

The factory is situated on the edge of Nantes. Today it looks like a regular fortress; successive barricades control the entry into the factory area. Every 20 meters there are picket lines (21 in all), ready to respond to any attack from the outside. Thugs from the C.D.R. (Committee for Republican Defense, a right-wing group) were expected that evening.

The CGT has the majority at Sud-Aviation with 800 votes, then comes the CFDT with 700 votes, then the CGT-FO with 300 votes. CGT pickets are suspicious of contacts with students; the worker-student link is made at point I6, the picket of the hourly FO workers, who have taken a revolutionary syndicalist line.

It all began with a demand for shorter hours without lower wages. After management refused to consider the workers' demands, the CGT and the CFDT called for a slow-down on May 1, the FO demanding an unlimited strike with factory occupation. May 7, two days before the first full day of the strike, the boss fled, pursued by 35 workers. He succeeded in getting away. May 10, discussions with management degenerated into a farce. The unions' policy of striking every half hour was reaffirmed by a vote which also rejected the CGT and FO proposal for a total strike without factory occupation.

---

39. This preferatory note was written by the editors of the journal in which this article appeared.

Tuesday, May 14, the half hour strikes continued, but around 3 P.M. three union delegates decided to chase the white collar employees out of their offices and to lock the boss in his office. Some white collar employees joined the sequestered boss. A guard was set up in front of his door. To keep the boss from getting bored, a loudspeaker playing ear-splitting revolutionary songs was installed next to his door, which no doubt enabled him to learn the *Internationale* by heart without ideological strain. But the sound was so loud it annoyed the union guard in front of the office as much as the director; the loud speaker was finally taken away, the musical concert ended.

A Strike Committee was set up, representing the elected delegates of the guard posts. The workers set these posts up spontaneously, using lumber to build watch towers for the monitors behind the walls of the factory. The first night the workers slept in refrigerator packing crates. Several days later, after Séguy's condemnation of acts of sequestration, the sequestering of the boss posed problems for the CGT unionists. The CFDT was in favor of releasing Duvochel (the boss) in exchange for posting a bond. The FO faction was for continuing the sequestration. The majority of the workers opposed Duvochel's liberation, which threatened to demobilize a good number of them. A representative of the CGT leadership, Desaigne, arrived from Paris during the night. This speed of movement astonished the workers. Desaigne asked them with pride:

"Guess how I came?"

The workers replied: "By bicycle?"

"No," replied Desaigne.

"By car?"

"No."

"By train?"

"No, by plane," replied Desaigne proudly, to the astonishment of most of the guard post.

At the inter-union council the next day Desaigne took the floor, explaining that he came on his own initiative against the judgment of the Confederation, and requested the liberation of Duvochel. The Strike Committee took this intervention very badly; a CGT delegate even retorted that the problem of Duvochel's sequestration could not be posed by an outsider. Furious, Desaigne finally left and took the plane directly for Paris. The next day there was a vote for or against Duvochel's sequestration; the director's release was decided by 66.7 percent of those voting.

Several days later the strikers perfected a system of internal organization within the company to maintain the occupation. A daily canteen was set up with donated labor. Permanent night shelters were installed everywhere in the factory. Entertainment was organized and there was a carnival for the benefit of the Strike Committee on Sunday.

This type of factory occupation is unprecedented in the history of Sud-Aviation although there had been lock-outs several times at the factory: in 1957, when it was occupied by the police; in 1960 another lock-out lasted two weeks after a wage strike, and in 1962 as well.

With its 2800 workers the Sud-Aviation factory is one of the biggest companies of the region.

THE BEGINNINGS OF DIRECT MANAGEMENT OF THE FACTORIES

The deepest phenomena of these last weeks have undoubtedly passed unseen. Excitement or anxiety focused everyone's attention on the spectacular aspects to the detriment of more important changes. However, several newspapers briefly mentioned cases in which workers called into question the organization of their labor, for example: work pace, safety on the job, productivity. Workers began to envisage making changes on their own initiative at Péchiney, Donges, the C.S.F. in Brest, etc. Unfortunately, the news did not say much about these experiments.

It is essential now to reflect on the embryos of self-management developed by the workers in certain factories because they represent a higher level of consciousness as compared with traditional wage demands. No doubt one of the characteristics of the May days was the hesitation and ambiguity surrounding the choice of a central terrain of struggle: the CGT always tried to keep the struggle at the level of strictly quantitative improvements; the CFDT put forward the ideas of participation and co-management without transcending the mystifying ideal of Swedish socialism. On the other hand, the rank and file could be seen leaving the terrain chosen by the CGT, or giving a radical content to CGT slogans by putting into practice the idea of appropriation of the means of production by the workers.

UNION DEMANDS AND THE PROBLEM OF POWER

Recently some students have proclaimed themselves "the only revolutionaries" because they emphasized the refusal of the university hierarchy while, they would have us believe, the workers were ignoble reformists whose struggle was limited to union demands. Coming from privileged groups, this pretension deserves only a smile. But by contrast with the opposite and even more dangerous view, the experience of 1936 allows us to answer no to the question, "Can the workers irreversibly improve their life conditions within the framework of the existing regime?" The need to challenge the bourgeoisie is clearly expressed in this slogan, written on the walls of Nantes:

> "MASSIVE INCREASE IN WAGES WITHOUT A CHANGE IN THE ECONOMIC AND POLITICAL STRUCTURES =
> INCREASE IN THE COST OF LIVING AND A RETURN TO POVERTY SEVERAL MONTHS FROM NOW."

What interests us is the fact that this position was put into practice even if in too limited forms. Witness this leaflet of the Sailors' Strike Committee, which preceded a long list of material demands with four points that posed the question of power:

STRIKE COMMITTEE OF THE PORT OF NANTES:
OFFICERS AND SAILORS

DEMANDS

As preconditions for all discussions:

1) Repeal of the antisocial Ordinances and the Decree of July 31, 1963, limiting the right to strike;
2) Full payment for strike days;
3) No disconnecting of salaries and official guarantees for the future.
—Recognition of union freedoms within the company.
—Increased power and legal immunity for the Delegate.
—Creation of a Company Committee within the Autonomous Port.
—Paritary management of the Company by the Delegates to the Company Committee, while awaiting the democratic nationalization of the Merchant Marine.
—Granting real powers to the Company Committees and a large increase in their budgets, 5 percent minimum.
—Return to the 40 hour work week without lower wages.
—Equal vacation and food bonuses for officers and sailors.

—Granting the 13th month on a fixed date.
—Etc. . . .

And there were not just leaflets. . . .

CHALLENGING THE MANAGERIAL HIERARCHY

The imprisonment of directors was the first symptom. Duvochel, the boss at Sud-Aviation, was locked up for several days until he got his freedom from that other boss, Séguy, despite the will of the workers.

The CGT delegate Andrieu told how sailors in the Merchant Marine rebelled for the first time against their commander. He was denounced and insulted because of his bad habit of spying on the private life of his men. Everything began with this act of disrespect. On another boat, a fake vote had been organized with the help of illiterate blacks to force a return to work. Immediately, thirty activists intervened and the subordinates put their chief in his place. A last example: this leaflet published by the Loire-Atlantique Social Security workers at the end of May demanding the repeal of the Ordinances:

In order to reach this goal as soon as possible, the departmental CGT and CFDT have agreed with their Confederations to immediately set up Provisional Management Committees composed entirely of wage earners in the department's various Social Security and Family Subsidy Funds.

These Committees are substituting themselves on their own initiative for the Councils set up by the Government in the framework of the Ordinances.

They are working rapidly to take the measures necessary to assure the election of Administrators from among the wage earning population, which is the only group qualified to manage funds belonging to the workers.

Management changed still more profoundly at the E.D.F. (Electricity of France) thermic center in Cheviré. Sunday, June 2, the day when I talked with the workers and technicians of this factory, they had just received an average raise of 15,000 old francs a month and . . . they continued the strike! This was because, as one of them said: "The executives have not been here for two weeks and the plant still runs. We don't need them to provide current." This intervention led to a whole discussion of the executive problem. They explained to me that in the Loire-Atlantique impressive numbers of executives were in solidarity with the workers, something never before seen. But support for wage demands was not the main point; the theme of management cemented the union. The executives were frustrated by the excessive centralization of public enterprises; they remain in their offices, signing papers, but they have no decision-making power.

Whether or not executives participated, what kind of self-management resulted?

THE FUNCTIONING OF DIRECT MANAGEMENT

We found the first stage in the organization of the factory occupations. Here, for example, is the communiqué of the Central Strike Committee concerning the A.C.B. ship yards:

On the third day of the occupation, the Central Committee was satisfied to observe the will to struggle of the whole A.C.B. personnel. No problems in the organization of rounds and rotations have been brought to the attention of the Committee. All shops, all offices are now well organized; this is worthy of note. When workers run things, they know how to get organized. Pay was distributed normally Wednesday at 4:00 P.M. Some comrades have not yet picked up their envelopes; to do so they should contact the Central Committee (tel. 322).

Canned goods were distributed after wages, and we take note of the personnel's self-discipline because all the orders were for less than 30 Francs, as requested.

The last two paragraphs give interesting hints about food supplies and the way in which accounts were settled among the workers themselves. Similarly, the strikers in the merchant marine requisitioned all the goods stored on the boats. This had never happened in earlier strikes, and this time too the ship owners tried to prevent the store rooms from being opened, but they had to yield in the face of threats to pry off the doors and locks.

Self-management was a necessity for the workers in the case of the Cheviré factory. When, on Saturday, May 18, the 293 agents occupied the place, they chose a strike committee composed of delegates from each union (90 percent of the workers at the E.D.F. are unionized).

While cutting back the current (which contributed to paralyzing local industries), they had to maintain a minimum of electricity to assure vital services: hospitals, etc. The Strike Committee therefore asked the strikers to "accept their responsibilities" in this domain. At the time of my investigation, the elected Committee had been the only source of authority in the plant for two weeks. The Committee saw to it that workers were there around the clock. It organized the continued supply of natural gas. It put order into the active but somewhat confused solidarity with which the surrounding population distributed food to the strikers.

The activists with whom I talked were very conscious (even the CGT delegate!) of the political meaning of this experiment, and one of them explained: "We wanted to show our ability and thus our right as producers to manage the means of production which we use. We've shown it can be done!"

If May 1968 was truly a "peaceful 1905" as Andrieu says, the 1917 to come will have to draw the logical consequences of these managerial conquests: power to the worker.[40]

FROM ROADBLOCKS TO SELF-DEFENSE

Nantes: May 24–May 31.

In the second half of the month of May official politicians and "leftists" debated whether the French situation was revolutionary or not. The debate is obviously much clearer in Nantes, where the state of the struggle is such that no one can avoid taking a stand. Here is a concrete example from a leaflet signed UNEF-Transportation FO, distributed on May 30:

CRS AGAINST ROADBLOCKS
On May 29, around 5 P.M., the Transportation FO and students organized a roadblock at the entrance of Sorinières. About

---

40. The reference here is to the two Russian Revolutions, the smaller and inconclusive one of 1905 foreshadowing the decisive events of 1917 that led to the establishment of a communist government.

50 oil drums were set up in the middle of the road by about 100 FO teamsters, helped by students.

In agreement with the Central Strike Committee, only private cars and trucks containing perishable goods with a pass from the Central Strike Committee were allowed through.

Then around 10 P.M., four busloads of Mobile Guards arrived from Nantes with six motorcycle policemen, not to mention the accompanying police cars. After calling the leader of the road-block, the chief of the forces of law and "order" ordered the attack, without warning.

There were several wounded, among them one high school student who was severely injured.

Those who wrote the leaflet and those who read it all agreed on the following facts: there is a Central Strike Committee; this Committee is in power; it decides on the right to travel on the roads; when private parties want to speak to someone in authority, they do not go to the Mayor or the Prefect but to the Central Committee. If this is not a revolutionary situation, when is there a revolution? Or do words no longer have any meaning?

Anyway, when the teamsters went on strike in Nantes, they did not ask subtle questions about revolution but they did see clearly that they had to control the communication of Nantes with the outside world. This was the only solution.

The roadblocks around Nantes were set up on Friday, May 24. The striking teamsters sealed off the main thoroughfares with the help of reinforcements of high school and college students. After May 26, the FO union—which dominates transportation in Nantes—acted in accord with the Central Strike Committee that had just been formed. The Central Strike Committee was already distributing gas rations; in addition, it was responsible for delivering permits to truckers to let only those goods through that were needed by the farmers or to supply the strikers with food. It was a good idea, but unfortunately confusion reigned at first due to a lack of organization. The Central Strike Committee distributed the permits badly because it had no competent "transportation" commission. No one wrote on the pass the number of the truck and the nature of freight (whether it was urgent or non-urgent merchandise). At first many truckers did not know that they needed a permit. The chief of the main "sweat shop" Grangjuoan, obtained a permit because the Central Strike Committee had not contacted the truckers! Etc. . . . In spite of this, the roads were controlled. The four main accesses were watched by pickets of 500 truckers and students. Those who tried to run the blockade suffered a few broken windows and flat tires, but there was no looting: on Saturday, June 1, an FO communiqué denied rumors concerning the ransoming of private cars. The cops did not dare to disperse their forces to attack. The city authorities became more or less complicit with the organization that had been established.

And so, for several days, a whole town was isolated, the blockades functioning as filters. They even prepared for armed resistance in case the meager police forces that were still at the disposal of the Prefect tried to intervene. However, from May 31 on the situation changed. The awakening of the Gaullist state made the threat of police repression real. The Pentecostal holidays had a demobilizing influence and the probable return to work in a few factories forced the unions to reinforce their picket lines, which reduced their strength on the roadblocks.

And finally, from fear of motorists' discontent, the Central Strike Committee decided on June 1 to abandon the system of gas rationing (which required a whole administration of 40 people). Under those circumstances, the roadblocks could no longer be held; they were dismantled the night of June 1. The battlefield had to be changed to avoid bloodshed.

As an FO delegate told me on June 2, "If Paris starts up again on Tuesday, escorted convoys of trucks will arrive en masse on June 4. No question of holding the roads! But if our picket lines in the factories prevent the trucks from being unloaded the struggle will continue."

Nantes will thus have lived for a week in a situation of semi-self-defense, which did not take a violent form only because public authority was dismantled.

FROM SELF-ORGANIZATION TO
SELF-MANAGEMENT

Just as during the Commune of Paris, the city of Nantes organized itself without having recourse to the intermediary bodies of the State.[41] From the first days of the strike on, the withering away of the State was

---

41. The Commune of Paris in 1871 abolished the city government and established a new type of governing body that combined legislative and executive functions. Representatives were responsible for carrying out the measures they passed. They could be recalled at any time. This model inspired later libertarian Marxist and anarchist thinking on the "withering away of the state."

realized in reality. To confront the situation, worker and peasant unions took control of the city's destiny.

This exemplary action has shown the masses of the people one of the most important things of all, namely that they have the capacity for self-organization. One element of socialism was concretely realized in the Nantes area, going far beyond the democratic reforms supported by the political parties. The Central Strike Committee, which brought together farmer and worker unions, moved into City Hall on Sunday, May 27. The Prefect had only a bailiff at his disposal.

I. Birth of the New Power: From Neighborhood Committees to the Central Strike Committee

Everything started in the Batignolles at the end of the second week of the strike (May 24). This is a 95 percent working class neighborhood of Nantes. The wives of the strikers there, mobilized by their family associations, decided to organize food distribution. Going through the neighborhood with a loudspeaker, the strikers' wives called the population to a meeting.

This first meeting was very enthusiastic and very militant; everyone was conscious of the political nature of the intended action. After the meeting, a delegation of about 100 strikers' wives went to the nearest factory to contact the Strike Committees.

A food supply committee was created, bringing together the three workers' family associations. This committee opened direct contacts with the farmers' unions of the nearest village: La Chapelle-sur-Erdre. A meeting of 15 unionized farmers and a delegation of workers and students decided to set up a permanent liaison to organize a distribution network without middlemen.

Simultaneously, on May 26, the unions discussed the establishment of a Central Strike Committee. This initiative had been demanded for a week by the U.O.FO of the Loire-Atlantique, which espoused revolutionary politics in opposition to the FO National Confederation.

This choice forced the unions to decide between blocking production completely or the use of the means of production by the producers in order to begin to create an autonomous people's power. The Central Strike Committee was composed of seven unions: the three workers' unions, the two farmers' unions (ENSEA, CNSA) and the two university unions (FEN, UNEF). There were two delegates from each union.

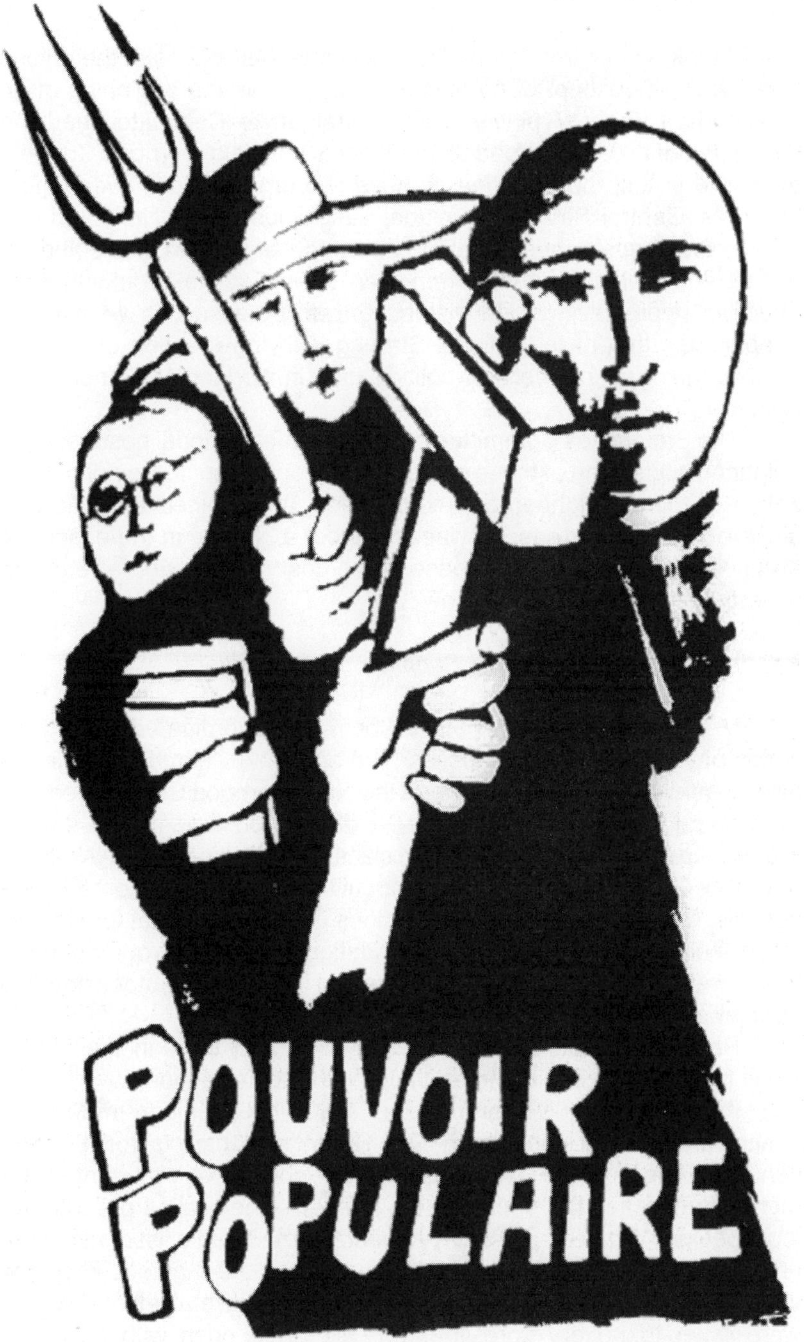
POUVOIR
POPULAIRE

It took a long time for the Departmental Assemblies of the unions to accept this concept of organic unity, but it was the beginning of an independent workers' power. The Central Strike Committee had the same idea of organizing food distribution as the Neighborhood Committees, and in fact the activities of these two organizations overlapped.

The Central Strike Committee, suspicious of the Neighborhood Committees, reproached them with having bypassed it in the beginning. In fact, the Neighborhood Committees turned out to be much more effective at organizing food distribution, and their action went much deeper than that of the unions. Starting with the creation of a direct market, they became cells of politicization in working class neighborhoods.

The Batignolles Committee put up four informational posters in the neighborhoods. One of those posters was proof of the degree of politicization of these neighborhood committees; it contained the following slogan: "Massive increase in wages without a change in the economic and political structures = increase in the cost of living and a return to poverty several months from now."

II. The Organization of Food Supplies by the Strikers

Meanwhile, the Central Strike Committee coordinated the organization of the various food supplies. The occupied Chamber of Agriculture maintained the liaison between the Neighborhood Committees and the Central Strike Committee. The Neighborhood Committees spread like wild-fire throughout the working class neighborhoods. On Wednesday, May 29, the Central Strike Committee opened six stores in the schools. On May 23, the farmers' unions issued an appeal for worker-farmer solidarity to organize food distribution concretely. Worker-student teams were created to help the farmers and they hoed potatoes and dug up the new potatoes.

Regular transportation was assured at first through the use of small trucks in the beginning and later with municipal buses.

Prices were equivalent to cost, a liter of milk going from 80 to 50 centimes, a kilo of potatoes from 70 to 12 centimes, carrots from 80 to 50 centimes. The big shop owners had to close down. Every morning union members checked the prices on the markets. They called out with the loudspeaker: "Shopkeepers, stay honest." Armed with a list of minimum and maximum prices, flying teams spread over the markets. Explanations were demanded of those who exceeded the maximum. Posters were issued to grocery stores that were allowed to open, with the following message: "Out of concern for the population's food supply, the unions allow this small shop to open its doors on the condition that it respects normal prices."

The farmers gave two and a half million [old] francs, which was kept in reserve in order to assure later survival. Many gifts in kind were added to that.

The workers left the electric current on, specifically to keep the dairies in operation. The fuel and gas needed by the farmers was delivered normally. Strikers delivered industrial food for cattle to the farmers.

In each of these actions, worker-farmer mutual aid was realized concretely with a clear consciousness of its political character. The transformation of agricultural techniques and the proletarianization of the farmers had created a new class of farmers in the younger generation who linked their destiny directly with that of the working class. The farm leader, Bernard Lambert, was the best representative of this new revolutionary consciousness among farmers.

III. The Generalization of Direct Management

On the other hand, the Central Strike Committee had also taken over the distribution of gas in agreement with the Oil Tankers' Strike Committee; rations were issued by the unions to the Health Services and the food distributors. This decision in no way called into question the strike action in the sectors concerned; it was limited to the organization of priority services under union control, which reinforced the power of the union in the city.

Unionized teachers and camp leaders organized nurseries for the strikers' children. The educational institutions' Strike Committees accepted responsibility for taking in the children and so avoided the collapse of the teachers' strike movements. At the same time, child care was organized in the universities.

Finally, the union organizations distributed food rations to the families of those strikers in the worst financial situation. These rations were the equivalent of a certain amount of food. For each child under three years of age, a ration of one franc for milk, and for each person older than three years, a ration of 500 grams of bread and a ration of one franc worth of food staples.

The small shopkeepers' unions and the pharmacists' unions collected the rations, which were payable at the cashier of the social aid bureau. The shopkeepers were asked to honor the rations out of solidarity with the strikers' families.

This direct organization by the new power implied the existence of a united political front between farmers, the working class, students and the middle classes. This united front was realized in Nantes and that is what made it possible to go on to the second level of the struggle: the creation of an autonomous workers' power in the face of the disintegration of the power of the ruling class.

Nantes was a unique, concrete example which demonstrated the possibility of a workers' government founded on direct management of the economy by the producers.

This testimony has drawn lessons directly from the May Events: if the unions and the workers' political parties had exploited the possibilities of the social movement, this second stage in the struggle could have been reached not only in Nantes, which is now just an example, but in every industrial city in France.

BIBLIOGRAPHY

Books

Altback, Philip G. *The Student Internationals*. New Jersey: Scarecrow Press, 1973.

Altback, Philip G. *Student Political Activism: An International Reference Handbook*. New York: Greenwood Press, 1989.

Aronowitz, Stanley. *False Promises*. New York: McGraw-Hill, 1973.

Atack, Margaret. *May '68 in French Fiction and Film: Rethinking Society, Rethinking Representation*. Oxford: Oxford University Press, 1999.

Benjamin, Walter. *Illuminations*. New York: Schocken, 1968.

Bourges, Herves. *The Student Revolt: the Activists Speak*. London: Cape, 1968.

Brooks, Gary D. *The Literature on Student Unrest*. Englewood Cliff, N.J.: Educational Technology Publications, 1970.

Burg, David F. *Encyclopedia of Student and Youth Movements*. New York: Facts on File, 1998.

Califano, Joseph. *The Student Revolution: a Global Confrontation*. New York: Norton, 1969.

Capdevielle, Jacques. *Mai 68 Soixante-Huit—L'entre Deux de la Modernité: Histoire de Trente Ans*. Paris: Presses de la Fondation Nationale des Sciences Politiques 1970.

Cogniot, Georges. *Les Etudiants et les Intellectuels Devant la Révolution*. Paris (imprimé d'institut Maruice Thorez), 1968.

Cohn-Bendit, Daniel. *Le Grand Bazar*. Paris: Belfond, 1975.

Couton, Andre. *Huit Siècles de Violence au Quartier Latin*. Paris: Stock, 1969.

De Certeau, Michel. *La Prise de la Parole*. Paris: Deselée de Brouwer, 1969.

DeGroot, Gerald J. *Student Protest: the Sixties and After.* London: Longman, 1998.

Delion, André G. *L'éducation en France: Problèmes et Perspectives.* Paris: Documentation Française, 1973.

Drane, Charles. *Les Grandes Heures de la F.E.A.N.F.* Paris: Chaka, 1990.

Dreyfus-Armand, Genevieve. *Mai '68: Les Mouvements Etudiants en France et dans le Monde.* Nanterre: Bibliothèque de Documentation Internationale Contemporaine, 1988.

Dubois, P. et al. *Grèves Revendicatives ou Grèves Politiques?* Paris: Anthropos, 1971.

Ehrenreich, Barbara. *Long March, Short Spring: the Student Uprising at Home and Abroad.* New York (Monthly Review Press), 1969.

Episemon. *Ces Idées qui ont Ebranlé la France (Nanterre, Nov 1967—Juin 1969)/Comprendre les Etudiants.* Paris: Fayard, 1968.

Faure, Christine. *Mai '68: Jour et Nuit.* Paris: Gallimard, 1998.

Feuer, Lewis Samuel. *The Conflict of Generations: the Character and Significance of Student Movements.* New York: Basic Books, 1969.

Fraser, Ronald. *A Student Generation in Revolt.* London: Chatto and Windus, 1988.

Glucksmann, André. *Stratégie et Révolution en France 1968.* Paris: Christian Bourgois, 1968.

Gretton, John. *Students and Workers: An Analytical Account of Dissent in France, May-June 1968.* London: Macdonald & Co, 1969.

Guin, Yannick. *La Commune de Nantes.* Paris: Maspero, 1969.

Hamon, Herve and Patrick Rotman. *Génération.* Paris: Seuil 1975.

Harvey, Sylvia. *May '68 and Film Culture.* London: British Film Institute.

Joffrin, Laurent. *Mai 68: Histoire des Evénèments.* Paris: Seuil, 1988.

Kerr, Clark. *The Uses of University.* Cambridge: Harvard, 1963.

Le Goff, Jean-Pierre. *Mai '68: L'Héritage Impossible.* Paris: La Decouverte.

Lefèbvre, Henri. *L'Irruption de Nanterre au Sommet.* Paris: Anthropos, 1968.

Lévy, Michel Louis. *Interdit d'interdire: les Murs de Mai '68.* Paris: Esprit Frappeur, 1998.

Linhart, Virginie. *Volontaires Pour L'usine; Vies d'établis, 1967–77.* Paris: Editions du Seuil, 1994.

Lipset, Seymour Martin. *Students in Revolt.* Boston: H. Mifflin, 1969.

Luxemburg, Rosa. "The Mass Strike, the Political Party and the Trade Unions." *Rosa Luxemburg Speaks.* M. A. Waters, ed. New York: Pathfinder, 1970.

Mallet, Serge. *La Nouvelle Classe Ouvrière.* Paris: Seuil, 1963.

Mallet, Serge. *Le Pouvoir Ouvrier.* Paris: Anthropos, 1971.

Marcus, Greil. *Lipstick Traces.* Cambridge: Harvard, 1989.

McGuigan, Gerald F. *Student Protest.* Toronto: Methuen, 1968.

Morin, Edgar and Jean-Marc Coudray (pseudonym of Cornelius Castoriadis). *La Brèche.* Paris: Fayard, 1968.

Perrot, Jean-Claude. *Les Sorbonne Par Elle-Même, Mai-Juin 1968; Documents.* Paris: Les Editions Ouvrières, 1968.

Prévost, Claude. *Les Etudiants et le Gauchisme.* Paris: Editions Sociales, 1969.

Reader, Keith. *The May 1968 Events in France: Reproductions and Interpretations.* New York: St. Martin's Press, 1993.

Rohan, Marc. *Paris '68: Graffiti, Posters, Newspapers and Peoms in the Events of May 1968.* London: Impact Books, 1988.

De Saint-Just, Louis Antoine. *L'Esprit de la Révolution.* Paris: UGE, 1963.

Schnapp, A. and P. Vidal-Naquet. *La Commune Etudiante.* Paris: Seuil, 1968.

Schnapp, A. and P. Vidal-Naquet. *The French Student Uprising.* Boston: Beacon, 1971.

Servan-Schreiber, J. *Le Réveil de la France.* Paris: Denoel, 1968.

Singer, Daniel. *Prelude to Revolution.* New York: Hill and Wang, 1970.

Spender, Stephen. *The Year of the Young Rebels.* London: Weidenfeld and Nicolson, 1969.

Spiegel, John. *The Dynamics of University Protest.* Chicago: Nelson-Hall, 1977.

Statera, Gianni. *Death of a Utopia: the Development and Decline of Student Movements in Europe.* New York: Oxford University Press, 1975.

Sur, Jean. *68 Forever.* Paris: Arlea, 1998.

Tartakowski, Danielle. *Les Manifestations de Rue en France et dans le Monde.* Paris: Publications de la Sorbonne, 1997.

Touraine, Alain. *Le Mouvement de Mai ou le Communisme Utopique.* Paris: Seuil, 1968.

Touraine, Alain. *Lutte Etudiante.* Paris: Seuil, 1978.

Weber, Henri. *Vingt Ans Après: Que Reste-t-il de 68?* Paris: Seuil, 1988.

Journal Articles

Baynac, Jacques and Herve LeBras. "Le Mystère 68." *Débat* 50 (1988): 61–78.

Boudon, Raymond. "Sources of Student Protest in France." *Annals of the American Academy of Political Science* 395 (1971): 139–149.

Debord, Guy. "Parisian Radicals of May 1968 Situationism." *The Economist* 347 (1998): 77–78.

Debouzy, Marianne. "The Americanization of the French University and the Response of the Student Movement." *American Studies International* 28 (1990): 23–36.

Decker, Jane E. "Direct Democracy and Revolutionary Organization in the 1969 French Student-Worker Revolt." *Proceedings of the Annual Meeting of the Western Society for French History* 5 (1977): 406–414.

Delannoi, Gill. "Mai et les Sciences Sociales dans l'Evolution Idéologique de l'Après-Guerre." *Cahiers de l'Institut d'Histoire du Temps Présent* 11 (1989): 27–37.

Garaudy, Roger. "Sur 'Mai Etudiant' et Sur la Philospophie de Lenine." *Pensée* 145 (1969): 15–20.

Jalabert, Laurent. "Aux origines de la génération 1968: Les Etudiants Francaises et la Guerre du Viêtnam." *Vingtième Siècle* 55 (1997): 69–81.

LePuloch, Maryvonne. "Les Années '68: Evénèments, Cultures, Politiques et Modes de Vie." *Bulletin de L'Institut d'Histoire du Temps Present* 63 (1996): 26–30.

McCreary, Eugine. "Film and History: New Wave Cinema and '68." *Film and History* 19 (1989): 61–68.

Prost, Antoine. "Quoi de Neuf Sur le Mai Français." *Mouvement Social—France* 143 (1988): 91–97.

Rovan, Joseph. "L'OFAJ a Seulement Vingt-Cinq Ans." *Documents* 3 (1988): 72–75.

Seidman, Michael. "Workers in a Repressive Society of Seduction: Parisian Metallurgists in May-June 1968." *French Historical Studies* 18 (1993): 255–278.

Singer, Daniel. "Twenty Years On: May '68 Revisited." *Monthly Review* 40 (1988): 18–37.

Witfield, Lee C. "The Rise of Student Political Power and the Fall of French Imperialism in North Africa." *Proceedings of the Annual Meeting of the Western Society for French History* 18 (1991): 515–523.

INDEX

189